The 21st Century Workforce

HANDBOOK FOR MANAGING TELEWORKERS

A 5-Step Management Process for Managing Teleworkers

By:

Sandra Gurvis

Don Philpott

Government Training Inc.™

Published by
Government Training Inc.™
www.GovernmentTrainingInc.com

Government Training Inc.™

About the Publisher – Government Training Inc. ™

Government Training Inc. provides worldwide training, publishing and consulting to government agencies and contractors that support government in areas of business and financial management, acquisition and contracting, physical and cyber security and grant writing. Our management team and instructors are seasoned executives with demonstrated experience in areas of Federal, State, Local and DoD needs and mandates.

Recent books published by Government Training Inc. ™ include:

☐ The COTR Handbook, 2010

☐ The Grant Writer's Handbook, 2010

For more information on the company, its publications and professional training, go to www.GovernmentTrainingInc.com.

Government Training Inc. ™

Rights and Contracts Department

5372 Sandhamn Place

Longboat Key, Florida 34228

Don.dickson@GovernmentTrainingInc.com

ISBN: 978-0-9844038-2-0

CONTENTS

About the authors

Sandra Gurvis

Sandra Gurvis (www.sgurvis.com), professional development instructor for Government Training Inc (GTI), is the author of fourteen books and hundreds of magazine articles. Her titles include MANAGING THE TELECOMMUTING EMPLOYEE with Michael Amigoni (Adams , 2009), MANAGEMENT BASICS, 2nd ed (Adams , 2007), and CAREER FOR CONFORMISTS (Marlowe, 2001), which was a selection of the Quality Paperback Book Club. Her books have been featured on "Good Morning America," "CBS Up to the Minute," "ABC World News Tonight," in USA Today and in other newspapers and on television and radio stations across the country; and have been excerpted in magazines.

Sandra has traveled throughout the US , lecturing and providing information on telework and telecommuting, as well as other issues relating to management and self-employment. She lives in Columbus, Ohio.

Don Philpott

Don Philpott serves as Publishing Editor for Government Training Inc. and has been writing, reporting and broadcasting on international events, trouble spots and major news stories for more than 40 years.

For 20 years he was a senior correspondent with Press Association -Reuters, the wire service, and traveled the world on assignments including Northern Ireland, Lebanon, Israel, South Africa and Asia.

He writes for magazines and newspapers in the United States and Europe and is a contributor to radio and television programs on security and other issues. He is the author of more than 90 books on a wide range of subjects and has had more than 5,000 articles printed in publications around the world. Among his most recent books include The COTR Handbook and The Grant Writer's Handbook – both published by Government Training Inc.

He is a member of the National Press Club.

Note from the Author

I've been working from home since Generation X was in diapers, including my own daughter Amy, who is now a thirty-something herself. Back in 1979, it wasn't known as "telework" but rather a "hobby to prevent Mom from losing her mind." The only people who were in business for themselves were professionals (such as doctors or lawyers), entrepreneurs, or franchisers. Except for the occasional consultant (then, as now, sometimes a buzzword for the terminally underemployed) most the rest of the jobs were in offices, factories, or other on-site locations. As a female professional, it was hard to be taken seriously; women either stayed at home full time or worked in offices. In an era when we were supposed to have it all, I was somewhere in between.

Today, of course, all that has changed. In my condo complex alone (and in the neighborhood where I lived in the late 1990s) about 20 percent of the residents work from their home offices. Who would have thought back in 1979 that I would have as much-if not possibly more-job security than some of my peers whose positions have been downsized or abolished?

Now that teleworkers are such a force themselves – and I myself sometimes employ them when my writing business gets busy – I realized there was a major need for a book on how to implement a management system. And as a former government employee who also worked in personnel, I wanted to come up with a step-by-step plan to simplify the acclimation to telework, helping it become the norm and acceptable (and comfortable!) to all levels of managers and employees.

Sandra Gurvis

Symbols

Throughout this book you will see a number of icons displayed in the margins. The icons are there to help you as you work through the Five Step process. Each icon acts as an advisory – for instance alerting you to things that you must always do or should never do. The icons used are:

Must Do   This is something that you must always do

No No   This is something you should never do

Tips   Really useful tips

Remember   Points to bear in mind

Checklist   Have you checked off or answered everything on this list?

FOREWORD – IT'S GREEN AND IT'S GROWING; TELEWORK IS HERE TO STAY

Overview

Teleworking, sometimes called telecommuting or flexiplace, is an innovative business solution that enables employees to do productive work away from the traditional office. Modern technological advances have made it easier to work anytime and anywhere.

Teleworking is a practical solution to environmental and other quality-of-life issues, as well as work-life challenges. The Office of Personnel Management (OPM) and General Services Administration (GSA) are lead agencies for the federal teleworking initiative. The GSA Government-wide Telework Team serves as the nexus for policy development, outreach, and collaborative partnerships to further the advancement of telework throughout the federal government. The Telework Team provides a variety of services, such as:

Developing policy concerning the alternative workplace

Promoting telework to and networks with federal, private, and other customers

Offering technical support, consultation, research, and development to its customers

Telework clearly has important implications for individuals and even entire communities.

Remember

Programs have been shown to help individual employees successfully balance the responsibilities of work and family, increase the safety of neighborhoods – as more people are home during the day – and reduce pollution. The potential benefits of a teleworking workforce are now more important than ever: with the cost of gas again on the rise, it has become a critical tool in the struggle to balance stretched family budgets; with the threats of new strains of influenza, it provides an effective resource in the face of possible pandemic; as our nation searches for ways to conserve energy, telework provides a valuable asset toward establishing green workplaces.

The Federal Situation

Late 20th-century technology revolutionized the workplace, and the 21st-century workplace is evolving even faster. Computers, remote connectivity, voice and electronic communications, paperless work processes, and other innovations make information and work increasingly mobile.

Such innovations help the federal government, as the nation's largest employer, serve the needs of the American public more efficiently and effectively. Federal employees have used mobile work technology for a long time. In recent years, telework has become increasingly widespread and formalized, with legislative mandates, as well as new programmatic and policy supports and structures.

The OPM defines telework as "work arrangements in which an employee regularly performs officially assigned duties at home or other worksites geographically convenient to the residence of the employee." Telework is simply a way of getting work done from a different location. It can serve multiple purposes – and have multiple benefits – when it is implemented effectively in an organization.

For federal agencies, telework is of particular interest for its benefits in the following areas:

- ☐ Recruiting and retaining the best possible workforce – particularly newer workers who have high expectations of a technologically forward-thinking workplace and any worker who values work/life balance
- ☐ Helping employees manage long commutes and other work/life issues that, if not addressed, can have a negative impact on their effectiveness or lead to employees leaving federal employment
- ☐ Reducing traffic congestion, emissions, and infrastructure impact in urban areas, thereby improving the environment
- ☐ Saving taxpayer dollars by decreasing government real estate costs
- ☐ Ensuring continuity of essential government functions in the event of national or local emergencies

Legislative Background

For over a decade, laws addressing telework (under various names – "work at home," "flexible work," "telecommuting," etc.) have been in effect for federal employees. The main legislative mandate for telework was established in 2000 (§ 359 of Public Law 106-346). This law states that "[e]ach executive agency shall establish a policy under which eligible employees of the agency may participate in telecommuting to the maximum extent possible without diminished employee performance." Associated language in the conference report for this legislation expanded on that requirement:

Each agency participating in the program shall develop criteria to be used in implementing such a policy and ensure that managerial, logistical, organizational, or other barriers to full implementation and successful functioning of the policy are removed. Each agency should also provide for adequate administrative, human resources, technical, and logistical support for carrying out the policy.

Further legislation (Public Law 108-199, Division B, § 627 of January 23, 2004, and Public Law 108-447, Division B, § 622 of December 8, 2004) followed this mandate with directives to certain agencies to increase telework participation in the workforce by specified amounts. As part of this congressional mandate, OPM began to survey federal agencies about telework in 2000. This Call for Telework Data collects information about agency programs and participation rates.

Definitions/Types of Telework

The terms "telework," "telecommuting," "flexible workplace," "remote work," "virtual work," and "mobile work" are all used to refer to work done outside of the traditional onsite work environment. These terms are defined in different ways and used in different contexts to refer to anything from jobs that are completely "virtual" or "mobile," to arrangements that enable employees to work from home a few days per week or per month.

OPM uses the term "telework" for reporting purposes and for all other activities related to policy and legislation. OPM defines telework as "work arrangements in which an employee regularly performs officially assigned duties at home or other work sites geographically convenient to the residence of the employee."

Telework arrangements in the federal government are most often part-time rather than full-time, although full-time telework does exist. Agencies may, at their own discretion, define and use the types of telework that best fit their business needs. However, for purposes of reporting and judging progress towards meeting the legislative mandate, OPM will count employees whose telework frequency is in one of the following categories only:

☐ Regular/recurring at least three days per week

☐ One or two days per week

☐ Less often than once a week, but at least once a month

As defined by OPM, telework is not –

Work extension: Many employees take work home with them. This is remote work, but it is not considered
Remember telework within the scope of the legislation.

Mobile work: Some agencies have employees who, by the nature of their jobs, are generally offsite, and may even use their home as their "home base." Because their work requires this setup and they travel much of the time, they are not considered teleworkers. This is different from "hoteling" arrangements, in which frequent teleworkers use shared space when they are onsite.

Telework is not an employee right. Federal law requires agencies to have telework programs, but does not give individual employees a legal right to telework.

The Current Position

The most recent report of the OPM's annual Call for Telework Data indicates a steady, albeit very slow, progress in telework, said Director John Berry. "In a recent Memorandum for Heads of Executive Departments and Agencies, I committed OPM to moving the Federal Telework Program forward through a series of important initiatives. The first of these have been met with the establishment of an expert Advisory Group that draws upon the knowledge of several leaders of high-performing telework programs. The results of this group's efforts will be used to help federal agencies develop strong consistent telework policies and, ultimately, effective telework programs. We have significant work ahead to develop a strong telework culture. I look forward to our continued collaboration with agencies on this important issue as we move telework forward in the federal government."

In February 2009, 78 executive branch agencies submitted data on their telework programs to the OPM. These data represent telework participation and related activities between January 1 and December 31, 2008.

Agencies have been submitting these reports to OPM since 2001, tracking the progress of telework implementation as the agencies have created and refined their programs and policies. Trends have remained relatively stable over time, with incremental increases and occasional decreases showing overall slow but steady growth.

For 2008, agencies reported that:

☐ 102,900 employees were teleworking

□ 64 percent of these employees were teleworking relatively frequently (either one-two days a week, or three or more days per week)

□ Almost half of the agencies had not fully integrated telework into their Continuity of Operations (COOP) planning

□ Office coverage and management resistance were considered the largest barriers to implementation

Data are reported for each of the agencies, and the large Cabinet-level agencies also report data at the sub-agency level. A closer look at the agency and sub-agency data allows us to break down the overall numbers to identify organizations that have experienced relatively large increases or decreases, either in actual participation or possibly in their capabilities to effectively track participation.

OPM continues to use these results and other information to support agency staff with their telework programs by convening regular meetings of telework coordinators, meeting one-on-one to provide consultation and support, maintaining the comprehensive www.telework.gov Website, and connecting agency staff so they can learn from each other's challenges and successes.

The Big Picture: Telework in 2008

□ 78 agencies reported a total of 102,900 employees out of 1,962,975 teleworking

- 5.24 percent of the total population reported as teleworkers
- 8.67 percent of the eligible population reported as teleworkers

□ 48 agencies (61 percent) reported an increase in their overall telework numbers

□ 78 percent of agencies provided formal notice of eligibility to their employees

□ 35 percent tracked the number of telework requests that were denied; 33 cases were due to performance or conduct issues, 160 were due to type of work

□ 38 percent tracked the number of agreements that were terminated; 108 of these terminations were based on the employee's decision, 31 were based on the supervisor's decision due to a performance/conduct issue, and 78 were based on a supervisor's decision due to a change in work assignments

□ 23 percent of agencies used electronic tracking to count teleworkers, 83 percent used telework agreements, 53 percent used time and attendance (note: agencies could select more than one category due to difference in tracking mechanisms at the sub-agency level, so the total exceeds 100 percent)

□ 44 agencies had fully integrated telework into COOP (56.41 percent)

☐ 27 agencies reported cost savings/benefits as a result of telework; of these, the greatest benefit was to morale (24 agencies), then productivity/performance and transportation (22 each), then human capital (21) (note: agencies could select all that apply)

☐ In terms of major barriers to telework, office coverage was highest (48 agencies), followed by management resistance (38), organizational culture (36), and IT security and IT funding (both at 25) (note: agencies could select all that apply)

☐ To overcome these barriers, 42 agencies were offering training for managers, 35 were offering training for employees, 29 had increased marketing, and 21 had established or increased budget for IT expenditures (note: agencies could select all that apply)

Comparisons to 2007

☐ Overall number of teleworkers increased from 94,643 in 2007 to 102,900 in 2008 (8,257 more teleworkers, an increase of 8.72 percent)

☐ Number of eligible employees decreased from 1,242,104 to 1,187,244

☐ Percentage of eligibles teleworking increased from 7.62 percent to 8.67 percent

☐ Percentage of total employees teleworking increased from 5.12 percent to 5.24 percent

☐ Frequency of telework rose:

- Number of employees teleworking three or more days/week increased, from
- 12,286 to 13,365
- Number of employees teleworking one-two days/week increased, from 45,231 to 52,339
- Number of employees teleworking at least once a month stayed basically the same (37,196 in 2008, 37,126 in 2007)

Specific Agency Information

☐ The Central Intelligence Agency, Office of Science and Technology Policy (Executive Office of the President), Peace Corps, and United States Holocaust Museum did not report

☐ Some agencies with substantial increases in total number of teleworkers:

- Department of Health and Human Services (11,272 to 12,785)
- Department of Interior (6,624 to 10,759)
- Department of Transportation (4,511 to 6,705)
- Department of Veterans Affairs (1,788 to 4,161)
- General Services Administration (1,727 to 4,754)

- National Labor Relations Board (224 to 368)
- Nuclear Regulatory Commission (268 to 442)
- Patent and Trademark Office (3,612 to 4,395)

☐ Some agencies with substantial decreases in total number of teleworkers:

- Department of Commerce (3,966 to 2,979)
- Department of Defense (17,921 to 16,871)
- Department of Justice (2,848 to 1,753)
- Department of State (2,447 to 1,004)
- Department of Treasury (6,861 to 5,444)
- Social Security Administration (4,011 to 3,440)
- U.S. International Trade Commission (149 to 64)

☐ Some sub-agencies with substantial increases in total number of teleworkers:

- Department of Commerce, Bureau of the Census (12 to 276)
- Department of Health and Human Services, Centers for Medicare and Medicaid Services (1,524 to 2,742)
- Department of Interior, U.S. Geological Survey (4,750 to 8,857)
- Department of Transportation, Federal Highway Administration (773 to 1,869)

☐ Some sub-agencies with substantial decreases in total number of teleworkers:

- Department of Agriculture, Food Safety and Inspection Service (891 to 364)
- Department of Commerce, National Oceanic and Atmospheric Administration (2,816 to 1,473)
- Department of Education, Office for Civil Rights (128 to 4)
- Department of Health and Human Services, Food and Drug Administration (3,813 to 2,670)
- Department of Justice, Executive Office for U.S. Attorneys (1,362 to 35)
- Department of Treasury, Office of Comptroller of the Currency (1,660 to 270)

Today, telecommuting is a flexible, inexpensive and safe option for many employees, with a host of benefits for employers, employees and the environment alike. So why aren't more people telecommuting?

Teleworking and IT Security

IT security involves protecting information and information systems from unauthorized access, use, disclosure, disruption, modification or destruction. It also ensures that system, data, and software integrity are maintained; and that information and system resources are protected against unplanned disruptions of processing that could seriously impact mission accomplishment.

There are many concerns, but IT security tops them all, with 42 percent of federal IT professionals and 27 percent of private-sector IT professionals saying that their top reservation about telecommuting is IT security, according to the fourth annual Telework Report from CDW Government (CDW-G). Despite their high confidence in the effectiveness of their security systems and in the federal government, tougher security standards appear to be reducing the number of employees eligible to telecommute.

According to the survey, private-sector employers have taken significant steps to expand telework initiatives, and private-sector telework adoption is approaching the federal level, with 14 percent of employees in the private-sector teleworking, compared to 17 percent of federal employees.

Federal agencies remain strong advocates for telework with 56 percent of federal IT professionals indicating that their agencies provide IT support for teleworkers. Since 2005, federal IT support has grown 23 percent, according to a year-over-year trend analysis of telework survey data.

Federal law requires agencies to enable telework for 100 percent of eligible employees. Drivers for federal telework adoption include military base closings and realignments, traffic congestion around major metropolitan areas and environmental impacts, as well as enabling productivity for field workers and planning for continuity of operations in the event of natural or manmade catastrophes.

Alongside the increase in technical support for teleworkers, the percentage of federal employees eligible to work remotely dipped to 40 percent from its high of 55 percent in 2006. The drop coincides with continuing concern about IT security.

"More stringent IT security policies are controlling telework expansion in the federal government," said CDW-G's Andy Lausch. "Federal agencies recognize that IT security and telework can co-exist, and they are carefully managing telework programs hand-in-hand with layered technology solutions that protect data and networks, while enabling the increased productivity and flexibility that telework affords."

Overall, IT professionals appear confident in their organizations' IT security measures. Eighty-four percent of federal IT professionals and 88 percent of private-sector IT professionals said their organization's IT security procedures and systems are effective. Fifty-six percent of federal agencies and 74 percent of private-sector employers authenticate teleworkers separately from their remote computers, ensuring that they know not only what devices are accessing their networks, but also who is at the keyboard. Moreover, nearly 70 percent of federal and private-sector employers are providing the computers and other equipment teleworkers use, providing an additional measure of control.

Despite those security protections, the survey revealed a gap in awareness that could introduce security weaknesses: 21 percent of federal employees and 31 percent of private-sector employees say they are not aware of their organization's corporate security policies, potentially opening the door to behaviors that risk security breaches.

Some Industry Perspectives

Telework Capability Benefits Continuity Planning, Employee Recruitment

Ever-heightening concerns about traffic congestion, air pollution and gasoline prices increase the attraction of telework, and the report also finds that the telework option could improve employee recruitment, satisfaction and retention. In fact, 50 percent of federal employees and 40 percent of private-sector employees say that the option to telework would influence their decision to remain with their employer or take a new job.

Further, broad telework adoption could ensure the continuity of government and business operations in the aftermath of a major catastrophe, or even for the duration of a minor disruptive event, such as a snowstorm, tornado or wildfire – and the latest survey finds mixed news on that topic. Consistent with the decrease in federal telework eligibility, federal employees' ability to continue to work remotely in the event of a natural or human-made disaster has declined significantly since 2007, with 59 percent of federal employees indicating that they could telework during a disruption, down from 75 percent in 2007. In the private sector, continuity of operations capability increased but still trails the feds, with 46 percent of employees indicating that they could continue working during a disruption, up from 33 percent in 2007.

The value of telework to continuity of operations is clear, with more than half of federal employees who can continue working during a disruption indicating that they are eligible to telework. In the private sector, the benefit is even more dramatic, with more than 70 percent

of employees who can continue working indicating that their company has a telework program.

"The private sector is solidly embracing telework. Continuity of operations alone could justify the investment, and improved employee satisfaction is icing on that cake," said Ken Grimsley, Vice President of Strategic Sales for CDW-G. "Still, many businesses remain unprepared for recovery from disruptions or are failing to take advantage of affordable, advanced security technologies that are justifiable even without telework. We have a long way to go."

Effective Communications

Remember Maintaining reliable, effective employee communication lies at the heart of successful telework programs, enabling the collaboration necessary to support continuation of essential government operations. Videoconferencing, which is already in place in nearly every federal agency, provides this essential connection – enabling virtual face-to-face interaction in a highly effective, reliable and cost-effective communications tool to support a remote workforce, according to Joel Brunson, President of Tandberg Federal. "Everyone agrees that teleworking is a great thing. The agencies focus on COOP [continuity of operations] and maintaining high performance; and employees are more aware of reduced travel times and improving their work balance."

Progress to teleworking, however, has been hindered by several factors. "Not so many years ago, equipment was cumbersome and expensive; with videoconferencing it was difficult to get through, and there was noise on the line. Now, with state of the art equipment and quality of service, together with lower prices on bandwidth, it is a much more positive situation," added Brunson. "Costs have come down so much that an agency can get a payback very quickly. Employers, however, still have to focus on changing the mentality that people have to be in the office in order to be effective. Out of sight does not mean out of mind, and it also doesn't mean that the worker is out of the office all the time. Managers must be trained to utilize teleworking by allocating appropriate time schedules," he said. "There is a wealth of research to show that teleworkers work longer hours and are more productive because they do not have to commute."

Security is the other permanent issue – everyone is frightened of it but it can be controlled. Manufacturers can control it by providing authentication and encryption, and agencies can control it by having the right policies in place. Ultimately it is everyone's responsibility to take security seriously, and this all comes down to training.

"Teleworking will become an even more lucrative option in the next few years because of the rising costs of fuel and commuting and even cheaper, more efficient equipment.

The government has to compete with the private sector for staff, and teleworking will be a significant factor in attracting new employees and retaining experienced people. This is an exciting time, but we have touched only the tip of the iceberg," he said.

Case Study

By mid-2001, officials in Concord, North Carolina, had developed a plan for training public safety employees, such as police and firefighters, through the use of video specialized training content communications. The purpose of the plan was to prevent a situation in which key personnel were in training sessions away from their precincts when an emergency call came in. To mitigate lag time in emergency response, training would be hosted from a central location, and participants would join in remotely through videoconference facilities at or near their respective stations.

After September 11, the need for such a system seemed even more urgent, as Homeland Security became a greater concern for first responders across the U.S. "The new Homeland Security effort helped to highlight the value of videoconferencing in a community like Concord," said Fire Chief Randy Holloway. "Instead of limiting its use to training, we could employ videoconferencing to a variety of communications challenges — both in response to a major crisis and in everyday applications."

The strategy tied together 31 video communication sites that would connect fire departments, police departments, emergency services, the public health department and the trauma center at the local hospital. What made the plan unique was that it included connecting all the same vital services of a nearby town, Kannapolis, into the same network. Additionally, Cabarrus County administration and four other municipalities had endpoint on the network, tying in an even larger and more dispersed geographical area.

The four municipalities, Harrisburg, Midland, Mount Pleasant and Locust, each had a TANDBERG video communications system installed at their local fire department. Adding to the region's emergency response capability in the event of a countywide disaster was the installation of three video systems at Emergency Operations Centers in Concord, Kannapolis and Cabarrus County facilities.

"In the event of a countywide disaster — whether hurricane, tornado or terrorist attack — leaders of each municipality can talk with each other via videoconference and make decisions together over secure, encrypted lines," Chief Holloway said.

Concord's proposal included the installation of a wireless network, which cost about $75,000. "With a wireless network, we avoid the recurring phone network costs, which were substantial," he explained. "Plus, the city owns it, so we are not dependent on the phone company or anyone else to keep the network operational."

According to Chief Holloway, there were several reasons for selecting TANDBERG. "Encryption technology was probably the most compelling issue," he said. "When you're talking about Homeland Security and the threat of some kind of terrorism, you need to know you have a secure network that can't be compromised during a crisis."

Around the time of the product testing, TANDBERG announced its intent to offer a bridge capable of conducting calls over Internet Protocol (IP), Integrated Services Digital Network (ISDN) or a mix of IP/ ISDN. In addition to providing secure calls for transmitting a variety of sensitive public safety information, this bridge supported encryption of calls in which patient names would be used, thus allowing compliance with the Health Insurance Portability and Accountability Act (HIPAA) standards for patient confidentiality — an important feature in daily use, as well as during a crisis.

"Sometimes, if I'm in my office during a three-alarm fire, or if a truck carrying hazardous materials crashes in a ravine, I can't see what's going on," Chief Holloway said. "With live video and two-way audio, I can more accurately assess the situation and make the best decisions about responses."

The City Council planned on using the network to allow citizens to participate in live council meetings from the fire department nearest their home and to use the network for training individual neighborhoods to be prepared for many kinds of emergencies. "If you take out the threat of terrorism and all the issues surrounding it," Chief Holloway said, "you have a network in place that will help citizens from one neighborhood connect with citizens in another neighborhood several miles away. They can say to one another, 'here is a problem we've had, and this is how we solved it.' This is a powerful way to link people together, to tie our city together, using the technology of videoconferencing."

According to Barry Leffew, Managing Director of Adobe's Public Sector enterprise team, the major problems preventing a faster uptake of teleworking are technical, cultural and security. "The challenges facing telework are similar to those found with other initiatives, namely Disaster Recovery, Continuity of Operations (COOP), Catastrophic Planning and Management, and even eLearning. Although technical, cultural, and security issues exist – the end user ultimately decides whether or not a system will be used. With that in mind, problems slowing the adoption curve relate to the 'user experience' and how quickly and easily the solution provides a benefit to the remote employee. If at any point employees find the solution more difficult than fighting traffic for two hours, we have failed," he said. To take it one step further, the user teleworking experience can be flawed by these technical and software issues:

Problem 1 – Hard to deploy: solutions only work in a single browser with a specified version running on one specific operating system given a specific service patch and installed with a particular thick client technology.

Problem 2 – Hard to use: regardless of how much training is done, users find it too difficult to do their job.

Problem 3 – Superiority complex: solutions fail to interoperate with "peer" systems; yet another stove-pipe is created.

"Selecting the 'right' technology for the enterprise is how to overcome these issues," continued Leffew. "We focus on a single concept – adoption. When an enterprise rolls out a solution that is easy to use, engaging, and fits within the enterprise architecture, we witness agency-wide adoption and a return on investment unlike anything else in the software space. We actually see communities embrace our technology and use it in ways originally not conceived. From our experience, it seems clear that the U.S. Patent and Trade Office (USPTO) is ahead of the curve in the Federal Civilian market," said Leffew.

Danette Campbell, the Senior Advisor for Telework, is a driving force for telework and has worked closely with the CIO's office to provide a set of technologies that enable remote work. Ms. Campbell's overall message on telework gives clarity to the mission: telework is part of a larger initiative, and benefits are witnessed across the board. For instance, transportation-demand management employs telework to reduce traffic, emissions, and cost. However, benefits are also found with employee satisfaction and retention. USPTO understands all of the relationships at play and realizes that this is a results-driven initiative.

The Department of Defense

In the Department of Defense, Defense Information Systems Agency (DISA) is leading the way with a number of telework initiatives to help deal with the upcoming Base Realignment and Closure Commission (BRAC).

It is clear that synergies exist between COOP and telework. Telework solutions represent the "everyday use" capability to a COOP plan. To be successful, COOP plans need to be exercised, measured and evolved. Because telework systems, policies, and players have a great deal of overlap with COOP systems, they can and should be used interchangeably. Instead of staging elaborate exercises and suffering from lost productivity, agencies like USPTO find themselves doing their job in more of an anywhere, anytime, any device mode as they telework. This sets them up for success if and when a COOP plan needs to be put in place.

It is not so much the specific advances in secure communications that make Telework possible today; instead it is the standards-based approach that software and hardware vendors are taking that allow us to easily assemble secure solution. These benefit telework within the Federal Civilian sector but are commonly used throughout the Department of Defense and Intelligence Communities.

Ultimately the pendulum continues to swing back towards the server with the Software as a Service (SaaS) models. This is a function of both back-end server technology, as well as widely deployed clients capable of so much more than today's browser. Although technologies like the Flash Player and the PDF Reader will continue to be a "face" to enterprise services, the new kid on the block is the Adobe Integrated Runtime (AIR). Adobe AIR promises the ideal end-user experience by fusing the best of the HTML, the Flash Player, and the Acrobat Reader. Companies, such as FedEx, eBay, and Citigroup have already started to invest in this Adobe AIR because it supports multiple platforms, allows for both online and offline transactions, provides rich and dynamic experiences, and is already being deployed at a global level.

Ultimately, the enterprise will be driven towards telework and COOP because of productivity. These initiatives will be seen as workforce enablement; telework isn't just a way to reduce commuting costs; COOP is not merely an insurance policy – it represents a strategic advantage.

Using This Guide

The back-to-back blizzards that hit Washington, DC, in February 2010, illustrate perfectly why teleworking is not just a good idea but critical. Following record snowfalls, more than 230,000 government employees were ordered to stay at home as the nation's capital virtually shut down for a week. Essential services were performed at offices around the country supported by thousands of Washington-based government employees who were able to continue working from their homes. Each snow day cost the government an estimated $100 million in lost productivity and related costs. Much money could have been saved if more federal workers had been trained and equipped to work from their homes. And if you factor the total expense of lost productivity in the commercial sector, the figures are even more staggering.

Remember
Teleworking is not only important; it is the wave of the future. This book is an A-Z guide aimed at managers tasked with introducing teleworking or overseeing teleworkers and ensuring that everything runs smoothly. The rules for managing teleworking are the same whether you are a federal or state employee or work for a private company or organization. Of course, the book should also prove to be very useful to people who are thinking of teleworking or trying to persuade their employers to introduce it.

The guide starts with an overview of what teleworking is, why it was introduced and what the current situation is. It then takes you through an easy to understand Five-Step Process which will help you determine whether teleworking is right for your organization and, if so, how best it can be implemented.

Step One gives you the tools you need to decide whether your organization needs teleworking. It looks at the jobs suitable for teleworking, the benefits and the technology needed to make it happen. Step One also tells you how to prepare a plan for implementation with advice on planning, policy and performance management.

Step Two focuses on putting together a teleworking team. This includes successful strategies for telework programs, creating guidelines for managers and employees, writing telework agreements and selecting and training the right people. There are also important sections on safety, security and the legal rights of teleworkers.

Step Three is all about organization – getting together a winning game plan. You will learn about virtual meetings, setting goals – and achieving them – organizing workflow and measuring productivity. In addition, there is more information about training and setting up a continuity-of-operations plan to maintain essential functions in the event of a major disaster.

Step Four covers implementation – how you make it all happen. There is information about setting up a home office, the equipment needed, how you establish communications procedures and how to manage by results. In addition, there is guidance on insurances, taxes and health care options and how they impact teleworkers.

Step Five talks about maintenance. You have set up your teleworking program, and this section is all about ensuring that the operation runs smoothly. You will lean about the importance of trust, performance evaluation and appraisals, how to reward your teleworkers and when to discipline them. There are also lessons for long-term success and how to grow teleworking in your organization. This last section also summarizes what you have learnt to become an effective telework manager if you have followed Steps One through Five.

Step One: Evaluation – Does Your Organization Need Teleworkers?

The Business Case for Teleworking

Remember

Teleworking is no longer an arrangement that only concerns certain managers and employees. It is an alternative that provides flexibility and good results in meeting organizational goals, as well as employee, customer and supplier needs. As a result, senior executives and managers are integrating teleworking as a strategic tool and making good use of teleworking benefits. For some employers, budgetary savings is a primary reason for initiating a teleworking program. For others, employee morale may be a top concern and incentive.

As the economy becomes more information based, teleworking continues to grow because work has become more portable. Individuals working in a variety of areas need not be located at a central base at all times. Also, real estate costs are rising and individual offices are shrinking. Computers and other communications technologies are increasing employee effectiveness and make teleworking easy and affordable. Remote technology has become more secure, available, and reliable. As long as teleworkers can communicate easily with their coworkers, managers, customers and suppliers, they can often work anywhere.

The most common objectives that organizations mention for introducing a teleworking program include:

- ☐ Attract new employees
- ☐ Retain key and quality employees
- ☐ Provide better service to customers, business partners, and suppliers
- ☐ Increase productivity and efficiency
- ☐ Provide a solution for peak periods and inconvenient working hours
- ☐ Ensure continuity of operations (COOP) in emergency situations and major disasters
- ☐ Reduce office space
- ☐ Reduce operating costs
- ☐ Establish a flexible, virtual networked organization

☐ Fulfill environmental responsibilities by decreasing the number of employees who may be commuting alone by car

Tasks Suitable for Telework

Telework can accommodate a wide range of tasks. Common examples include, but are not limited to:

☐ Independent Thinking and Writing

☐ Researching a topic

☐ Analyzing data

☐ Reviewing proposals or contracts

☐ Responding to correspondence

☐ Drafting reports or other documents

☐ Telephone Use

☐ Setting up a conference

☐ Obtaining information

☐ Following up with customers

☐ Computer Use

☐ Programming

☐ Graphic design

☐ Web page design

☐ Data entry

☐ Word processing

☐ Desktop publishing

While many tasks are suitable for telework, some tasks require the employee's physical presence in the office. Unsuitable tasks may include those that involve:

☐ Extensive face-to-face contact with the manager, coworkers, or other agency staff

☐ Access to systems, equipment, or material that cannot be moved from the office

☐ Safeguards and control due to security requirements

Tips

The ideal situation is to divide up the workweek so the telework-suitable tasks that can be done from a remote location, with the remainder being accomplished in the office. With that in mind, the exact number of telework days depends on four factors:

Step One: Evaluation – Does Your Organization Need Teleworkers?

- ☐ The manager's comfort level with how many teleworkers can be out of the office for how many days a week
- ☐ The teleworker's comfort level with the number of days he/she is willing to work remotely
- ☐ The needs of coworkers and clients
- ☐ Any limitations on office space availability in the central office and/or at a telework center

Now that you have made your decisions about what tasks are best suited for telework, the next step is to determine which people are likely to be good teleworkers. The easiest and fairest way would be to say that people who are doing their jobs well in the office and consistently meet performance expectations are the most eligible for telework.

Tips

What distinguishes a good teleworker? For starters, he/she typically:

Is able to work with minimal direct supervision

Has been in the job and department long enough to be able to solve many of his/her own problems and answer many of his/her own questions

Has demonstrated the ability to "deliver the goods" on time and according to specifications, and has effective time-management skills

Has demonstrated the ability to initiate and guide his/her own work and is the proverbial "self-starter" who does not need to be reminded to get the job done

Can and does communicate effectively with a variety of others, using a mix of personal and electronic means as is appropriate

By nature, teleworkers must be self-reliant, even if it's only one or two days a week. That's why employees who have demonstrated the ability to do what's expected with minimal direct supervision provide the greatest potential for teleworkers.

In any selection decision, past performance is the best predictor of future effectiveness. If you want to determine how likely it is that someone will self-motivate, meet deadlines, and do independent problem-solving, look for how well they have done it while working in the office.

However, even if you've identified the right tasks for telework, and the right person to do those tasks, there may still be reasons why a person should not telework from home. The home environment may have too many distractions and interruptions (e.g., if there are preschoolers running around or it lacks an area for a work space). That's where telework centers come in so well.

Remember

Identifying Teleworking Benefits

While many private and public employers initially created teleworking programs to address environmental mandates or enhance employee work/life balance, employers currently recognize many other benefits of allowing and enabling employees to telecommute. Teleworking has the potential to provide significant benefits for employers, employees and the community.

Checklist

Teleworking will help your organization in the following ways:

Productivity

☐ More Work Accomplished

♦ Greater Focus

♦ Fewer Distractions

☐ Job Satisfaction

♦ Improved Morale

♦ Greater Commitment/Loyalty

☐ Greater Efficiency

♦ Commute Time Savings

♦ Less Stress

♦ Flexible Work Schedule

Cost Efficiency

☐ Reduces Hiring and Replacement Costs

♦ Relocation Costs - Hiring Expenses

♦ Training Time and Expense

☐ Reduced Unscheduled Absences

♦ Less Down-Time

♦ Reduced Costs Associated with Unscheduled Absences

☐ Real Estate Savings

♦ Reduced Office Space

♦ Increased Parking Efficiency

♦ Shared Work Space

♦ Reduced Operating Expenses

♦ Controlled Expansion Expenses

Step One: Evaluation – Does Your Organization Need Teleworkers?

Flexibility

☐ Less Down-Time

♦ Ability to Work on Snow Days

♦ Ability to Work During Sick Leave

♦ Ability to Work Remotely

♦ Ability to Return to Work for Injured Employees

☐ Retention and Attraction

♦ Retention of Key Employees

♦ Retention of Employees Relocating

♦ Attraction of Employees Seeking Flexible Arrangement

☐ Wider Labor Pool

♦ Access to Workers in Larger Geographic Area

♦ Attract and Retain Qualified Persons with Physical Disabilities

☐ Less Absenteeism

♦ Ability to Work Without Infecting Others With Colds, Flu, and other Contagious Illnesses

♦ Ability to Work Outside of Traditional Office Hours

Teleworking will help your employees:

☐ Reduce Commute Time, Costs, and Stress

☐ Increase Job Satisfaction

☐ Increase Productivity

☐ Balance Work and Home Life More Easily

☐ Maintain Better Health

☐ Value, and Remain With, the Organization

Teleworking will help the community:

☐ Decrease Traffic Congestion

☐ Conserve Resources Through Reduced Gasoline Consumption

☐ Reduce Air Pollution

☐ Offer More Employment Opportunities for Untapped Labor Force (e.g., disabled, part- time, retired, work-time availability)

Source: Telecommute Connecticut! Best Practices Guide

Remember A telework program can benefit the employer in a variety of ways including enhanced recruitment/retention, reduced absenteeism, increased employee satisfaction and productivity, lower real estate costs and the ability to continue operations in the event of a natural disaster or human-made emergency. From a productivity standpoint, teleworkers report time and time again that they get more work done when working outside the office due to fewer interruptions.

In terms of organizational competitiveness, many employers report that teleworking has enabled them to attract and retain skilled employees because it provides the workplace with the flexibility they are seeking. In some cases, employers have been able to expand their "geographic reach" by hiring employees who live in other parts of the country without the need for relocation.

Reasons Companies Considered Telework Solutions

We were outgrowing our office space, but didn't want to move, so we chose a telework plan. Our employees think it's great, and productivity is up.

We didn't have enough parking. Our telework arrangement solved the problem, and our employees appreciate the flexibility.

Imagine if you no longer had to commute to work every day. Teleworking is a perk that employees love. In fact, it's so popular at our company that we've actually seen a decline in recruiting and training expenses.

The goal of our telework program was to attract and retain quality employees. We knew we would have a larger hiring pool if we offered the flexibility of working from home.

The Basics

The benefits of a telework program are widespread. According to the International Telework Association and Council, on average, teleworking yields:

☐ 22 percent increase in employee productivity

☐ 20 percent decrease in employee turnover

☐ 60 percent decrease in employee absenteeism

Some Common Myths and the Reality

Myth - All of my employees will want to telework.

Truth - Only about 20 percent of employees wish they could telework.

Step One: Evaluation – Does Your Organization Need Teleworkers?

Myth - Telework is a full-time arrangement.

Truth - Most employees only telework one-three days a week.

Myth - Teleworkers are out of sight, out of mind.

Truth - With modern technology teleworkers share seamless communication with their office and clients, at all times.

Myth - As a manager, how will I know the telework employees are actually working?

Truth - If your employees are communicating with you, and their assignments are completed on schedule, then your employees are working.

Myth - Teleworking is really just a substitute for dependent care.

Truth - Teleworkers have work to complete, and must arrange for dependant care just as if they were working in the office.

Myth - Teleworking and telemarketing are the same thing.

Truth - Teleworking is working remotely from a main office, while communicating with the workplace via email, phone, fax or modem. Telemarketing is the practice of selling goods or services over the phone.

Some of the Doubts Expressed by Management

Once I allow my employee to telework, I will never see or hear from him/her again.

Chances are you will only be dealing with part-time teleworkers in which employees will work at home or at a telework center one or two days per week. Create an environment where employees feel comfortable contacting you, and consider (especially at the outset) scheduling a daily telephone meeting with your teleworker just to check in on work progress. Let your employees know your expectations for their availability if you need to reach them while they are teleworking. Remember, if at any time you feel that a teleworker is not performing as you expected, you can modify or cancel the agreement.

Remember

If I approve one agreement, I will have to let all my employees telework.

No employee is entitled to telework; it is not a universal benefit available just for the asking. Each telework agreement should be treated independently. You should consider the requirements of each job or task and the performance of each employee requesting a telework arrangement. Your decision should be based on the merits of each individual request and on

maintaining equitable decision-making regarding telework, not simply on what was approved for someone else.

Telework stands in the way of effective teamwork.

Tips

Successful teamwork does not require all team members to be together in the same physical place. Effective work planning and communication strategies can support team efforts across time and space for a variety of job tasks and functions. Team members can work together to establish their own procedures for working together; typically these will include a mix of in-person meeting time, phone calls, conference calls, email, and perhaps other methods of working together without being together 100 percent of the time.

Worker productivity will drop if I am not watching my employees every minute.

Remember

Rather than experiencing declines in job performance, many organizations that encourage teleworking how improvements in productivity. At a minimum, you should expect telework to have little if any negative impact on productivity; that is, the amount or quality of work completed. Teleworkers should be just as productive working from home as they are in the office, assuming you have made the right decisions about which tasks and employees are best suited for telework. If you experience any reduction in productivity with a teleworker, you should work with him/her to identify the problem and solutions, which may include modification or cancellation of the telework agreement.

Work Planning/Scheduling Requirements

You will likely have to make some adjustments to how your office does business to accommodate telework. When your entire staff is in the office every day, it's easy to schedule impromptu meetings. If you have part-time or full-time teleworkers on staff, however, you may need to plan these meetings in advance and/or arrange for your teleworkers to participate via electronic means (telephone, videoconference, Web conference, etc). When making work assignments, you may also need to coordinate the assignments with your teleworkers' schedule. Teleworkers need to be flexible to accommodate your scheduling requirements.

Proximity in the office doesn't guarantee high effectiveness. Many managers of teleworkers report it is beneficial to have to pay more attention to scheduling meetings in advance, instead of always having the luxury of calling meetings on the spot. The latter are definitely necessary sometimes, but in most cases a bit of planning goes a long way in helping all staff members make the best use of their time.

The Benefits

Allow employees to be more effective: With the right tools and a flexible schedule, employees are able to work any time, anywhere, without the distractions of the office. This allows employees to be more focused and productive.

Increase management results: Managers with telework employees often have more efficient employees with higher-performance standards. Managing the results of your telework employees will help you to gauge the success of your program.

Ensure uninterrupted work: Without the need to commute, your telework employees escape the many delays associated with traffic and extreme weather. And, without the distractions of the office, teleworkers are better able to focus on their work.

Reduce real estate costs: When an employee teleworks two or three days a week, the empty office space offers options for desk-sharing and storage. This additional space can allow a company to grow without moving or adding costly real estate. Parking expenses are reduced and limited parking can be shared, lowering overhead even more.

Decrease employee recruitment and training costs: A flexible workplace raises morale and lowers turnover. Higher employee retention lowers company recruitment, hiring, and training expenses. Profitable companies seek the top employees and attempt to hold onto them. Job seekers want more than high pay – they want challenging, interesting, supportive and flexible work environments. Companies with a telework program have an obvious competitive edge.

Allow for business continuity: Teleworking can be a key component of a business continuity plan in the event of bad weather, a pandemic, or any other crisis that closes the central office location.

Lower relocation costs: In some cases, the cost of relocating employees can be avoided altogether by combining a telework arrangement with business travel.

Increase quality of life: The flexibility of working offsite allows employees to focus on work, without the stress of how to get there.

Lower personal costs: Telework employees spend less on their professional wardrobe, eating out, dry cleaning and transportation (including vehicle usage, gas, and insurance).

Expand the human resource pool: There's an untapped talent pool of qualified potential employees who are unable to drive. Teleworking can alleviate the need for

transportation altogether, allowing companies to hire these empowered, independent employees. The result is a telework staff with higher morale, work ethic, and company loyalty.

Benefit the environment: The fewer cars on the highways, the safer and healthier the environment. And companies can feel good about reducing their employees' dependence on oil.

Over the past decade, the notion of telework has sparked increasing interest among employees and employers alike, according to the Telework Exchange. According to the report "The Perfect Storm: Driving Telework in State and Local Agencies," major corporations, as well as the federal government, have established proven telework policies and procedures. In the federal government, Congress mandated agencies to adopt telework to both support work/life balance and also to provide a way to alleviate traffic congestion and to reduce vehicle emissions. As a result, Congress established Public Law 106-346 [Department of Transportation and Related Agencies Appropriations Act, 2001], which requires federal agencies to establish and promote telework programs for eligible employees. State and local governments, often considered behind the curve on telework, have the opportunity to adopt telework as mainstream operating practice and reap similar benefits.

Additionally, today's technology has finally enabled businesses and governments to effectively implement mobility and telework programs. No single technology breakthrough explains the progress. Rather, a series of step-by-step advances and steady investment in telecommunications networks, software, and computer processing have contributed to the telework growth. In particular, videoconferencing technology evolved to the point where teleworking can almost replace face-to-face interaction and communication, thus eliminating management's No. 1 telework concern – losing touch with employees.

Agency Benefits

Continuity of Operations (COOP): Business as Usual

! Must Do Responsible for initial response and recovery efforts in times of emergency, state and local agencies must continue to provide support to all constituents regardless of the circumstances. To do this, state and local agencies now find it imperative to incorporate telework into continuity of operations (COOP) plans. Information technology research firm Gartner, Inc., reports that agencies that implement teleworking as a primary work format stand the best chance to get their employees back to work as safely and quickly as possible. In addition, they are ideally positioned, via remote access, to move rapidly in the event of a disastrous interruption to operations. Rather than being a "break glass in case of an emergency" situation, telework must be implemented into agencies' standard operating procedures to reap the benefits.

Hennepin County, headquartered in Minneapolis, Minnesota, and serving more than 1.1 million people in 46 communities, is one local government that benefited from proper COOP planning and effective telework policy. Instead of shutting down the county government during the 2008 Republican National Convention, the county relied on its telework policy to maintain a "business as usual" workload. Implemented in 1997, this telework policy avoided what could have been a drastic break in business continuity.

Personnel Recruitment and Retention

A recent study by the Center for State and Local Government Excellence reported that 54 percent of the state government workforce and 57 percent of the local government workforce are between ages 40 and 61 and nearing retirement. Further, the National Association of State Chief Information Officers (NASCIO) found the option to telework to be an increasingly important bargaining chip between organizations and younger, Generation Y employees. Respondents placed workplace flexibility at the top of their list of what attracts new workers to state government employment – second only to benefits packages. Telework also allows state and local agencies to retain knowledgeable senior workers longer while recruiting younger employees who demand greater flexibility and more work/life balance.

Many state and local agencies already have robust telework programs that provide employees with more autonomy over where and when they work, without compromising product quality. Employees are looking for this kind of flexibility today and in the future.

Remember

Real Estate Savings

Telework is also a viable solution in reducing physical office space. Estimates in the private sector indicate that telework can cut corporate real estate costs as much as 90 percent. On the public-sector front, many federal agencies have relinquished their office space in favor of "hoteling" programs that reserve workspace for employees who come into the office. According to the Gartner research firm, while the actual reduction in office space depends on how employees use the space, the rental cost for the floor area, and the slight increase in shared office space for teleworkers, the average reduction is still roughly 130 to 140 square feet per remote user per year. The result is significantly reduced real estate maintenance and cost.

A telework program in Loudoun County, Virginia, recently expanded the traditional definition of telework to include mobile workers. The program provides county building inspectors with the tools to complete their tasks in the field and at home, without traveling to and from the office. The county has equipped building inspectors and supervisors, approximately 70 employees, with notebook computers containing broadband cards and

virtual private network (VPN) access to the county's network and its applications. Through the program, each inspector can receive assignments, conduct research, and communicate inspection results remotely, eliminating the twice-daily drives to and from the main office every workday. Loudoun County hopes to realize $95,000 in savings when the current office lease expires.

Employee Benefits

Work/Life Balance and Cost Savings

Telework Exchange finds that Americans spend more time commuting each year than on vacation. Telework can change that by reducing time in commuter traffic and offering greater flexibility to manage work/life balance. In Alabama's Department of Transportation, new hires throughout the state can now go to their nearest division office for training, rather than driving three or four hours to the central office in Montgomery. The state of Arizona estimates that its employees who telework drive 5.25 million fewer miles and endure 181,000 fewer hours of stress every year.

Telework can also significantly reduce travel costs, especially considering the fluctuating price of gas. Congestion wastes 2.9 billion gallons of gas in the United States each year, creating a $78-billion annual drain on the economy. Telework Exchange research finds that by teleworking full time, the average commuter can save more than $2,000 a year on gas alone. Telework Exchange offers Telework Value Calculators, available at www.teleworkexchange. com, that tally potential cost savings and environmental benefits associated with telework.

Conducting a Pilot Study

A pilot study is a mini version of a full-scale study and provides valuable insights into the feasibility of a given project. In the case of teleworking, a small-scale study can be useful to measure the attitudes of both the participating teleworkers and their managers, determine what equipment and software is needed, and help establish guidelines and operating protocols.

Pros and Cons of Conducting a Pilot Study

A pilot program is beneficial because:

☐ It tests telework as a concept without the cost of full implementation.

☐ It reveals who teleworking will impact and how.

☐ It allows a chance for managers who may be resistant to experience a "test" run.

☐ It reveals what is working about the program, and what changes need to be made.

The downside of a pilot program is that:

☐ It might prematurely doom a program before all the kinks are worked out.

☐ It delays the process of starting your program. Most pilot programs last anywhere from three months to two years, although there is no ideal time-frame.

☐ Those not chosen for the pilot program may become jealous or resentful.

How to Say No

No one likes to say "no," but there are times when you may have to: an employee may come to you with a telework proposal that's not feasible. How to handle these requests will depend on the particular circumstances in each case. In any event, be honest, equitable, and open to suggestions on how to turn the situation around.

!
Must Do

The three main reasons why you might have to turn down a telework proposal are:

☐ The employee's responsibilities are not suited to telework.

☐ Technical or budget limitations prevent you from approving it at this time.

☐ The employee lacks the appropriate work habits for telework, and/or has demonstrated work habits that do not suggest he/she is a good candidate for telework, e.g., repeated absences, lateness, missed deadlines, etc.

Technology: The Key to Telework

Technology – from available broadband to low-cost, high-performance collaboration tools – is paving the way for greater telework adoption. Telework technology requirements vary by agency – there is no "one-size-fits-all" approach. Agencies must purchase telework technology that best fits its employees' needs. In fact, most large organizations already have the technology needed to implement telework programs. Many teleworkers require a computer, associated peripheral equipment (e.g., printer, copier, scanner, facsimile), phone, Internet connectivity, secure network access (e.g., virtual private networks [VPNs]), and technical support. Further, many agencies are already using tools, such as video conferencing, Web-based collaboration solutions, voice over Internet Protocol (VoIP), and mobile personal digital assistants (PDA) to enhance the work environment and increase mobility.

Major advancements in collaborative technology can alleviate what 32 percent of federal managers list as their biggest concern about telework – a lack of natural, face-to-face interaction. Studies show that face-to-face communication is critical to building relationships,

reducing misinterpretations among dispersed teams, and removing misperceptions and barriers to telework.

As telework programs continue to gain momentum, new Web collaboration solutions and video conferencing systems are essential for home-based employees to maintain a visual connection with their workplace. Only since about 2007 has the availability of bandwidth for video technology evolved to make teleworking effective.

Video conferencing, as a component of all telework technology, is more than just a corporate expense; it is an investment in an organization's efficiency, productivity, and employee morale. Conferencing and collaboration solutions – with added capabilities, including application sharing, white-boarding, enhanced management tools, the ability to distribute meeting materials, the capability to record and playback sessions, and more – have finally joined the ranks of the telephone and email as core business tools that agencies need to function in today's world.

Preparing to Implement a Telework Program

While the benefits of telework may speak for themselves, management resistance, security concerns, and limited prior exposure to telework remain obstacles to successfully launching telework programs. Several key steps will ensure smooth implementation of a state or local telework program.

Test Drive Continuity of Operations: Test the agency's ability to telework in the event of an extended emergency situation to determine preparedness and the existence of robust business continuity plans.

❗ Must Do **Eliminate Management Resistance:** Educate management on the benefits of telework and how it will help their teams. Agencies should implement manager-specific pilot programs, educate all management levels on telework drivers and benefits, emphasize the importance of telework to COOP strategies, implement performance-based review processes, build support gradually with a phased rollout approach, and incorporate face-to-face technology solutions to ease concerns about management disconnect. Research finds that as managers' telework involvement increases, they express more favorable attitudes. Managers most involved in telework – i.e., those who telework themselves – report favorable impressions with 21 percent greater frequency than managers who do not telework or manage teleworkers.

Properly Allocate Resources: Provide at least one full-time, senior-level telework advisor to focus exclusively on implementing or expanding the telework program. Telework advisors must have the time to educate managers and employees about telework, provide necessary

training, and update agency telework policies. Also, ensure that advisors consult COOP planning teams, as well as IT personnel, when developing a telework program.

Implement Evaluation System: Develop measurements and evaluation forms to monitor the progress and tangible benefits of the telework program.

Address Security Requirements: Audit and understand the full population of teleworkers to ensure they are working within an official telework program. Establish and enforce security guidelines and provide training and technology to ensure a secure mobile environment.

Develop Policy and Eligibility Criteria: Develop an agency-wide telework policy and consistently define eligibility so all employees understand the criteria for teleworking. Make telework opt-out rather than opt-in for employees and their managers.

Five Phases of Planning and Implementation

Launching a telework program requires more than buying the right technology and sending staff to their home offices. Robust state and local telework programs align with the organization's mission, culture, and business requirements, to ensure teleworkers have suitable places to work offsite, and mandate that managers and employees have signed formal telework agreements. Success hinges on policies, procedures, training, and careful evaluation of the program.

A sound telework policy outlines specific technology requirements. Agencies must determine what equipment (if any) the organization will provide, offer reimbursements for Internet and phone charges, properly address security issues associated with the equipment, and provide guidelines on how teleworkers should solicit technical support. In addition, the policy must clearly define how an employee determines their telework eligibility. Tools, such as Telework Exchange's Eligibility Gizmo (www.teleworkexchange.com/gizmo), are available for managers to help determine telework eligibility.

Once the organization implements its policy, training becomes the single best strategy for avoiding pitfalls. Managers are trained to manage by results, not by constant supervision; non-teleworkers are trained in how to communicate with teleworkers; and teleworkers are trained in how to work remotely. Employees must be comfortable with their telework situation, and they must also be culturally and technologically ready to work outside of the office.

Remember

The final key to implementing a successful telework program is to establish measurable goals. As an example, the state of California measures teleworker and non-teleworker

performance against project schedules and key milestones, regular status reporting, peer and/ or project team quality reviews, team participation in decision making, and trust.

Following are the phases used to implement a telework program.

Phase 1: Initiation. This phase includes the tasks an organization should perform before it starts to design a telework or remote access solution. These include identifying needs for telework and remote access, providing an overall vision for how telework and remote access solutions would support the mission of the organization, creating a high-level strategy for implementing telework and remote access solutions, developing a telework security policy, and specifying business and functional requirements for the solution.

Phase 2: Development. In this phase, personnel specify the technical characteristics of the telework or remote access solution and related components. These include the authentication methods, the cryptographic mechanisms used to protect communications, and firewalls and other mechanisms used to control access to networks and their resources. The types of telework clients should also be considered, since they can affect the desired policies. The telework security policy should be employed and enforced by all clients. Solution components are procured at the end of this phase.

Phase 3: Implementation. In this phase, equipment is configured to meet operational and security requirements. This includes the telework security policy documented in the system security plan; it is installed and tested as a prototype, then activated on a production network. Implementation includes altering the configuration of other security controls and technologies, such as security event logging, network management, and authentication server integration.

Phase 4: Operations and Maintenance. This phase includes security-related tasks an organization should perform on an ongoing basis once the telework or remote access solution is operational, including log review and attack detection. These tasks and policies should be documented and configured by the appropriate management.

Phase 5: Disposal. This phase encompasses tasks that occur when a remote access solution or its components are being retired, including preserving information to meet legal requirements, sanitizing media, and proper disposal of equipment.

Phase 1: Initiation

The initiation phase involves many preparatory actions, such as identifying current and future needs and specifying requirements for performance, functionality, and security. A critical aspect is developing a telework security policy. This section describes what the policy

should contain and, where relevant, some factors to be considered when making the decisions behind each element.

The telework security policy should be documented in the system security plan. It should define which forms of remote access the organization permits, which types of telework devices are permitted, the type of access each type of teleworker is granted, and how user account provisioning should be handled. It should also cover how the organization's remote access servers are administered and how policies in those servers are updated.

Remember

In addition to the considerations described in this section for telework security policies, organizations should also consider how other security policies may be affected by telework. For example, an organization may require that certain types of locked-out user accounts may only be unlocked in person; however, this may not be viable for teleworkers on travel or on long-term offsite assignments. Other security policies should be adjusted as needed to take telework into consideration.

Permitted Forms of Remote Access

One of the first decisions to make when setting a teleworking security policy is to determine which types of remote access should be permitted. Each solution has its strengths and weaknesses, and the usefulness will depend on many factors within the organization. Some of those factors include:

Existing remote access used by the organization, such as remote control systems used by IT staff.

Software already installed on telework devices that can be used for remote access.

Capabilities available in firewalls already installed at the edge of the organization's network.

The types of remote access permitted for telework should be closely tied to the organization's overall security policy. If a certain form of remote access cannot be secured according to the organization's security policy, such as using approved cryptographic algorithms to protect sensitive data, then that form should not be used. The overall security policy should take priority when creating a telework security policy.

Restrictions on Telework Client Devices and Remote Access Levels

A telework security policy can limit the types of client devices that teleworkers are allowed to use for remote access. For example, an organization might permit the use of only organization-owned PCs. Some organizations have tiered levels of access, such as allowing

organization-owned PCs to access many resources, teleworker-owned PCs to access a limited set of resources, and consumer devices and third-party PCs to access only one or two resources, such as Web-based email. This allows an organization to limit the risk by permitting the most-controlled devices to have the most access and the least-controlled devices to have minimal access.

Remember Each organization should make its own risk-based decisions about what levels of remote access should be permitted from which types of devices. Factors to consider when setting telework security policy include the following:

Sensitivity of telework: Certain types of telework involve access to sensitive information or resources. Organizations with more restrictive requirements for telework involving sensitive information may permit the use of only organization-controlled telework devices.

The level of confidence in security policy compliance: Meeting many of an organization's security requirements can typically be ensured only if the organization controls the configuration of the telework devices. For personally owned devices, some requirements can be verified by automated security health checks conducted by a remote access server, but other requirements cannot be verified by automated means. Making users aware of their responsibilities can help improve security on personally owned telework devices, but will not result in the same degree of security policy compliance as mandatory security controls on organization-controlled telework devices. Even the most conscientious users may fail to properly maintain the security of their personally owned devices because of the technical complexity, the effort involved, or their lack of awareness of new threats.

Cost: Costs associated with telework devices vary based on policy decisions. The primary direct cost is issuing the devices and client software to teleworkers. Indirect costs include maintenance and providing technical support for teleworkers. Another consideration related to cost is telework frequency and duration; an organization might justify purchasing telework devices for regular or part-time teleworkers (e.g., one day per week from home, frequent business travel). However, costs are not justified under certain situations, such as when office-based individuals want to quickly check email from home a few evenings a month.

Telework location: Risks will generally be lower for devices used only in the home environment than for those in a variety of other locations. Also, in some cases the organization can automatically determine the teleworker's location (i.e., identify whether the device is on an authorized home network), making it easy to enforce location-based policies.

Technical limitations: Certain types of devices may be required for particular telework needs, such as running specialized programs. Also, if an organization has a single type of remote access server, and that server can only allow connections through a custom client, then only the types of devices that can support the client are allowed.

Compliance with mandates and other policies: Organizations may need to comply with telework-related requirements from mandates and other sources, such as a federal department issuing policy requirements to its member agencies. An example of a possible requirement is restrictions on performing telework in foreign countries that have strong known threats against federal agency systems.

Organizations may choose to specify additional security requirements tied to factors, such as the sensitivity of telework. Many organizations require more stringent security controls for high-risk situations. Helpful security requirements for telework may include the following:

Permit high-risk telework only from organization-issued and secured telework devices.

Require the use of multi-factor authentication for access to the telework device and to remote access solutions.

Use storage encryption on the telework device to protect all sensitive information. Multiple levels of encryption may be needed. For example, full disk encryption may prevent an attacker who gains physical access to the device; at the same time, virtual disk encryption or file/folder encryption may stop an attacker who gains logical access to the device (i.e., access after full disk encryption authentication has occurred and the data on the hard drive is being decrypted automatically). Removable media containing telework data should also be encrypted.

Migrate high-risk resources to secure servers that allow the telework access.

Store and access only minimum necessary data. Some organizations issue "loaner" devices that are completely wiped before and after performance of high-risk telework. Only the data and authorized applications needed for the telework are loaded onto the loaner device. The pre-use wiping ensures that the device is clean before any telework is conducted, and the post-use wiping ensures that no telework data remains that could be accessed in the future.

In high-risk situations, organizations may also choose to reduce risk by prohibiting telework and remote access involving particular types of data, such as highly sensitive personally identifiable information (PII).

Every year, there are many changes in telework device capabilities, the security controls available to organizations, the types of threats made to different types of devices, and so on.

Therefore, organizations should periodically reassess their policies regarding telework devices and consider changing which types of client devices are permitted and what levels of access should be granted. Organizations should also be aware of the emergence of new types of remote access solutions and of major changes to existing technologies, and ensure that the organization's policies are updated accordingly.

Additional User Requirements

Phase 1: Security

Organizations often have additional security considerations for telework that, while helpful in diminishing threats, cannot be directly enforced by the organization. For instance, the teleworker may download unauthorized files from the Website for personal use which could pose a security threat. Organizations should educate users on the importance of these additional security measures, and define teleworkers' responsibilities for implementing them in policy and telework agreements.

One example of a possible security consideration is phone services. For example, corded phones using traditional wired telephone networks cannot be intercepted without physical connections, so they are sufficiently secure for typical telework. Cordless phones using traditional wired telephone networks should employ spread spectrum technology to scramble transmissions, thus reducing the risk of eavesdropping within physical proximity (usually a few hundred yards at most). Digital cell phones should be acceptable for typical telework. Communications carried over Voice over IP (VoIP) services should not be considered secure unless some form of encryption is used; however, many VoIP services now provide strong encryption, which should be used to protect sensitive and proprietary information. Any encryption used must be certified to follow National Institute of Standards and Technology (NIST) requirements. The FIPS 140 specification, Security Requirements for Cryptographic Modules, defines how cryptographic modules are validated (http://csrc.nist.gov/publications/fips/fips140-2/fips1402.pdf).

Another possible security consideration involves wireless personal area networks (WPAN), which are small-scale wireless networks that require no infrastructure. Examples of WPAN technologies are using a wireless keyboard or mouse with a computer, printing wirelessly, synchronizing a PDA with a computer, and allowing a wireless headset or earpiece to be used with a cell phone. The two most commonly used types of WPAN technologies are Bluetooth and infrared. When not using them directly, teleworkers should disable these technologies to prevent unauthorized access.

Phase 2: Development

Once the organization has established a telework security policy, identified telework and remote access needs, and completed other preparatory activities, the next step is to determine which types of telework or remote access technologies should be used. The many considerations for designing a solution, most of which are generally applicable to any IT technology include the following:

Architecture: Designing the architecture includes the placement of the remote access server and the selection of remote access client software (if needed).

Authentication: Authentication involves selecting a remote access authentication method and determining how its client/user and server components should be implemented, including procedures for issuing and resetting authenticators and for provisioning users and client devices with authenticators.

Cryptography: Decisions related to cryptography include selecting the algorithms for encryption and integrity protection of remote access communications, and setting the key strength for algorithms that support multiple key lengths.

Access Control: This involves determining which types of remote access communications should be permitted and denied.

Endpoint Security: Endpoint security decisions involve determining how remote access servers and telework client devices should be secured.

The security aspects of the telework and remote access solution design should be documented in the system security plan. The organization should also consider and document how incidents involving the telework and remote access solutions should be handled, as well.

Phase 3: Implementation

After the remote access solution has been designed, the next step is to implement and test a prototype before putting the solution into production. Aspects of the solution to be evaluated include the following:

Connectivity: Users can establish and maintain remote access connections. Users can only connect to all of the permitted resources and no others.

Protection: Each traffic flow is protected in accordance with the established requirements. This includes flows between the telework client device and the remote access server, and

between the remote access server and internal resources. Protection should be verified by means, such as monitoring network traffic or checking traffic logs.

Authentication: Authentication is required and cannot be readily compromised or circumvented. All authentication policies are enforced. Performing robust testing of authentication is important to reduce the risk of attackers accessing protected internal resources.

Applications: The remote access solution does not interfere with the use of permitted software applications, nor does it disrupt the operation of telework client devices (for example, a VPN client conflicting with a host-based firewall).

Management: Administrators can configure and manage the solution effectively and securely. This includes all components, including remote access servers, authentication services, and client software. The ease of deployment and configuration is particularly important, such as having fully automated client configuration versus administrators manually configuring each client. Another concern is the ability of users to alter remote access client settings, which could weaken remote access security. Automating configurations for devices can greatly reduce unintentional errors.

Logging: The remote access solution logs security events in accordance with the organization's policies. Some remote access solutions provide more granular logging capabilities than others – for example, logging usage of individual applications versus only connections to particular hosts – so in some cases, reliance on the resources used through remote access are necessary to perform certain portions of the logging.

Performance: The solution provides adequate performance during normal and peak usage. Not only should the performance of the primary remote access components be considered, but also intermediate devices, such as routers and firewalls. Performance is particularly important to telework client devices during large software updates through the remote access solution. Encrypted traffic often consumes more processing power than unencrypted traffic, so it may cause bottlenecks. The best way to test a prototype performance under load is to use simulated traffic generators on a live test network. This will mimic the actual characteristics of expected traffic. Testing should also incorporate a variety of applications to be used with remote access.

Security of the Implementation: The remote access implementation itself may contain vulnerabilities and weaknesses. Organizations with high security needs may perform extensive vulnerability assessments. At a minimum, all components should be configured with and follow sound security practices and be updated with the latest patches.

Default Settings: Implementers should carefully review the default values for each remote access setting and alter the settings as necessary. Implementers should also ensure that the remote access solution does not unexpectedly "fall back" to default settings.

Phase 4: Operations and Maintenance

Operational processes are particularly helpful for maintaining telework and remote access security, and should be performed regularly; include the following:

Remember

Checking for upgrades and patches to the remote access software components, and acquiring, testing, and deploying the updates.

Ensuring that each remote access infrastructure component (servers, gateways, authentication servers, etc.) has its clock synched to a common time source so that its timestamps will match those generated by other systems.

Reconfiguring access control features as needed based on factors, such as policy changes, technology changes, audit findings, and new security needs.

Detecting and documenting anomalies within the remote access infrastructure. Such anomalies might indicate malicious activity or deviations from policy and procedures. If applicable, anomalies should be reported to other systems' administrators.

Organizations should also periodically perform assessments to confirm that the organization's remote access policies, processes, and procedures are properly followed. Assessment activities may be passive, such as reviewing logs, or active, such as performing vulnerability scans and penetration testing. More information on technical assessments for telework and remote access is available from NIST SP 800-115, Technical Guide to Information Security Testing and Assessment (http://www.itl.nist.gov/lab/bulletns/bltndec08.pdf).

Phase 5: Disposal

Before a telework client device or remote access server permanently leaves an organization, such as when a server's lease expires or when an obsolete PC is being recycled, the organization should remove any sensitive data. Data may also need to be wiped if an organization provides "loaner" devices to teleworkers, particularly for travel. The task of scrubbing all sensitive data from storage devices, such as hard drives and memory cards, is often surprisingly difficult because data resides in places other than just the user's data area. For example, software that runs under Microsoft Windows often stores possibly sensitive data

in the Windows registry. NIST SP 800-88, Guidelines for Media Sanitization (http://www.nist. org/nist_plugins/content/content.php?content.52) has recommendations on removing data from telework and remote access devices. In fact, the organization should strongly consider erasing all storage devices completely.

Organizations should document the security aspects of the telework and remote access solution design in the system security plan.

The policy should define the permitted forms of remote access, which types of telework devices are permitted, the type of access each teleworker is granted, and how user account provisioning should be handled. It should also cover how the organization's remote access servers are administered and how policies in those servers are updated.

Each organization should make its own risk-based decisions concerning the permissible levels of remote access for each telework client device.

Organizations should periodically reassess their policies for telework devices. Considerations include changing types of client devices and levels of access.

Before putting a remote access solution into production, an organization should implement and test a prototype of the design. Connectivity, traffic protection, authentication, management, logging, performance, implementation security, and interference with applications should all be evaluated.

Organizations should regularly perform operational processes to maintain telework and remote access security, such as deploying updates, verifying clock synchronization, reconfiguring access control features as needed, and detecting and documenting anomalies within the remote access infrastructure.

Organizations should also periodically perform assessments to confirm that the organization's remote access policies, processes, and procedures are properly followed.

Telework Security Policies and Controls

!
Must Do Plan telework security policies and controls based on the assumption that external environments contain hostile threats.

An organization should assume that external facilities, networks, and devices contain hostile threats that will attempt to gain access to the organization's data and resources. Organizations should assume that telework client devices, which are used in a variety of external locations and are particularly prone to loss or theft will be acquired by malicious

parties who will attempt to recover sensitive data from them. Options for mitigating this type of threat include encrypting the device's storage and not storing sensitive data on client devices. Organizations should also assume that communications on external networks, which are outside the organization's control, are susceptible to eavesdropping, interception, and modification. This type of threat can be mitigated, but not eliminated, by using encryption technologies to protect the confidentiality and integrity of communications, as well as authenticating each of the endpoints to each other to verify their identities. Another important assumption is that telework client devices will become infected with malware; possible controls for this include using anti-malware technologies, using network access control solutions that verify the client's security posture before granting access, and using a separate network at the organization's facilities for telework client devices brought in for internal use.

Develop a telework security policy that defines telework and remote access requirements.

A telework security policy should define which forms of remote access the organization permits, which types of telework devices are permitted to use each form of remote access, and the type of access each teleworker is granted. It should also cover how the organization's remote access servers are administered and how policies in those servers are updated.

As part of creating a telework security policy, an organization should make its own risk-based decisions about what levels of remote access should be permitted from which types of telework client devices. For example, an organization may choose to have tiered levels of remote access, such as allowing organization-owned personal computers (PC) to access many resources, teleworker-owned PCs to access a limited set of resources, and other PCs and types of devices (e.g., cell phones, personal digital assistants [PDA]) to access only one or two lower-risk resources, such as Web-based email. Having tiered levels of remote access allows an organization to limit the risk it incurs by permitting the most-controlled devices to have the most access and the least-controlled devices to have minimal access.

There are many factors that organizations should consider when setting policy regarding levels of remote access to grant; examples include the sensitivity of the telework, the level of confidence in the telework client device's security posture, the cost associated with telework devices, the locations from which telework is performed, and compliance with mandates and other policies. For telework situations that an organization determines are particularly high-risk, an organization may choose to specify additional security requirements. For example, high-risk telework might be permitted only from organization-issued and secured telework client devices that employ multi-factor authentication and storage encryption. Organizations

may also choose to reduce risk by prohibiting telework and remote access involving particular types of information, such as highly sensitive personally identifiable information (PII).

Information Security Issues

Your responsibilities as a manager concerning security issues of your teleworkers include:

Thorough review all telework agreements to ensure they are in compliance with agency information security policies.

Make sure that all employees receive agency information systems security training.

Work with all employees to ensure they fully understand and have the technical know-how.

Invest in technology and equipment that can support success.

Work with employees to develop secure systems for potentially sensitive documents and other materials.

Track removal and return of potentially sensitive materials, such as personnel records.

Enforce personal privacy requirements for records.

Work with all employees to ensure they fully understand and have the technical knowledge needed to telework.

Vulnerabilities, Threats, and Security Controls

All of the components of telework and remote access solutions, including client devices, remote access servers, and internal servers accessed through remote access, should be secured against a variety of threats. General security recommendations for any IT technology are provided in NIST Special Publication (SP) 800-53, Recommended Security Controls for Federal Information Systems. Specific recommendations for securing telework and remote access technologies are presented in this publication and are intended to supplement the controls specified in SP 800-53.

Telework and remote access technologies often need additional protection because their nature generally places them at higher exposure to external threats than technologies only accessed from inside the organization. Before designing and deploying telework and remote access solutions, organizations should develop system threat models for the remote access servers and the resources that are accessed through remote access. Threat modeling involves identifying resources of interest and the feasible threats, vulnerabilities, and security controls related to these resources, then quantifying the likelihood of successful attacks and their

impacts, and finally analyzing this information to determine where security controls need to be improved or added. Threat modeling helps organizations identify security requirements and design the remote access solution to incorporate the controls needed to meet the security requirements. Major security concerns for these technologies that would be included in most telework threat models are:

Lack of Physical Security Controls: Telework client devices are used in a variety of locations outside the organization's control, such as employees' homes, coffee shops, hotels, and conferences. The mobile nature of these devices makes them likely to be lost or stolen, which places the data at increased risk of compromise. When planning telework security policies and controls, organizations should assume that client devices will be acquired by malicious parties who will attempt to recover sensitive data. The primary preventative strategies are either to encrypt the client device's storage so that sensitive data cannot be recovered by unauthorized parties, or not to store sensitive data on client devices. Even if a client device is always in the possession of its owner, there are other physical security risks, such as an attacker looking over a teleworker's shoulder at a coffee shop and viewing sensitive data on the screen.

Unsecured Networks: Because nearly all remote access occurs over the Internet, organizations normally have no control over the security of the external networks used by telework clients. Communications systems used for remote access include telephone and Digital Subscriber Line (DSL) modems, broadband networks, such as cable, and wireless mechanisms, such as IEEE 802.11, WiMAX, and cellular networks. These communications systems are susceptible to eavesdropping, which places sensitive information transmitted during remote access at risk of compromise. Man-in-the-middle (MITM) attacks may also be performed to intercept and modify communications. Organizations should plan their remote access security on the assumption that the networks between the telework client device and the organization, including teleworkers' home networks, cannot be trusted. Risk from use of unsecured networks can be mitigated, but not eliminated, by using encryption technologies to protect the confidentiality and integrity of communications, as well as using mutual authentication mechanisms to verify the identities of both endpoints.

Infected Devices on Internal Networks: Telework client devices, particularly laptops, are often used on external networks and then brought into the organization and attached directly to the organization's internal networks. Also, an attacker with physical access to a client device may install malware on the device to gather data from it and from networks and systems to which it connects. A client device infected with malware may spread throughout the organization once it is connected to the internal network. Organizations should assume that

client devices will become infected and plan their security controls accordingly. In addition to using appropriate anti-malware technologies, such as anti-malware software on client devices, organizations should consider the use of network access control (NAC) solutions that verify the security posture of a client device. Organizations should also consider using a separate network for telework client devices, instead of permitting them to directly connect to the internal network.

External Access to Internal Resources: Remote access provides external hosts with access to internal resources, such as servers. If these internal resources were not previously accessible from external networks, making them available via remote access will expose them to new threats, particularly from untrusted client devices and networks. Each form of remote access that can be used to access an internal resource increases the risk of that resource being compromised. Organizations should carefully consider the balance between providing remote access to additional resources and the potential impact of a compromise of those resources. They should also ensure that any internal resources they choose to make available through remote access block external threats and that access to the resources is limited to the minimum necessary through firewalling and other control mechanisms.

For more information on Remote Access Methods see Appendix Nineteen. Appendixes can be found at http://governmenttraininginc.com/Managing-Teleworkers-110809.asp.

Protecting Devices

To support confidentiality, integrity, and availability, all of the components of telework and remote access solutions, including client devices, remote access servers, and internal servers accessed through remote access should be secured against a variety of threats.

Before designing and deploying telework and remote access solutions, organizations should develop system threat models for the remote access servers and the resources accessed through remote access.

When planning telework security policies and controls, organizations should assume that client devices will be acquired by malicious parties who will attempt to recover sensitive data from the devices.

Organizations should plan their remote access security on the assumption that the networks between the telework client device and the organization, including teleworkers' home networks, cannot be trusted.

Organizations should assume that client devices will become infected with malware and plan their security controls accordingly.

Step One: Evaluation – Does Your Organization Need Teleworkers?

Organizations should carefully consider the balance between the benefits of providing remote access to additional resources and the potential impact of a compromise of those resources. Any internal resources made available through remote access should be hardened against external threats; access to the resources should limited through firewalling and other access control mechanisms.

When planning a remote access solution, organizations should carefully consider the security implications of the remote access methods in the four categories – tunneling, portals, remote desktop access, and direct application access – in addition to how well each method may meet operational requirements.

Ensure that remote access servers are secured effectively and are configured to enforce telework security policies.

Remote access servers provide a way for external hosts to gain access to internal resources, so their security is particularly important. In addition to permitting unauthorized access to resources, a compromised server could be used to eavesdrop on and manipulate remote access communications, as well as to provide a "jumping off" point for attacking other hosts within the organization. Organizations need to ensure that remote access servers are kept fully patched and that they can only be managed from trusted hosts by authorized administrators. Organizations should also carefully consider the network placement of remote access servers; in most cases, a server should be placed so that it acts as a single point of entry to the network and enforces the telework security policy.

Secure telework client devices against common threats and maintain their security.

Many threats to telework client devices include malware and device loss or theft. Generally, telework client devices should include all the local security controls used in the organization's secure configuration baseline for its non-telework client devices. Examples are applying operating system and application updates promptly, disabling unneeded services, and using anti-malware software and a personal firewall. However, because telework devices are generally at greater risk in external environments, additional security controls are recommended, such as encrypting sensitive data stored on the devices and adjusting existing security controls. For example, if a personal firewall on a telework client device has a single policy for all environments, then it is likely to be too restrictive in some situations and not restrictive enough in others. Whenever possible, organizations should use personal firewalls capable of supporting multiple policies and configure the firewalls properly for both the enterprise and an external environment.

Organizations should ensure that all types of telework client devices are secured, including PCs, cell phones, and PDAs. For PCs, this includes physical security (for example, using cable locks to deter theft). For devices other than PCs, security capabilities and the appropriate security actions vary widely by device type and specific products, so organizations should provide guidance to device administrators and users responsible for securing telework consumer devices.

Telework Client Device Security

Telework client devices can be divided into two general categories:

Personal computers (PC), desktop and laptop computers running standard PC operating systems (OS), such as Windows 7, Vista, and XP; Linux/Unix; and Mac OS X.

Consumer devices, which are small, usually mobile computers. Examples of consumer devices are networking-capable PDAs, cell phones, and video game systems. Consumer devices are most often used for Web-based remote access, such as portals or direct access to applications, but consumer devices are increasingly supporting other forms of remote access, as well. Consumer devices are often owned by individuals, but some types of devices are frequently owned and distributed by organizations.

The gap between PCs and consumer devices is closing. Some current consumer devices run standard PC operating systems, but these are often not intended for users to direct access. Also, consumer devices are increasingly offering more functionality previously provided only by PCs.

Another set of categories is the party responsible for the security of the client device. These categories are as follows:

Organization: Client devices in this category are usually acquired, configured, and managed by the organization. These devices can be used for any of the organization's remote access methods.

Teleworker: These client devices are owned by the teleworker, who is ultimately responsible for securing them and maintaining their security. These devices are usually capable of using many or all of the organization's remote access methods, if permitted.

Third party: These client devices are owned, configured, and secured by third parties, such as kiosk computers at hotels, and PCs or consumer devices owned by friends and family. Remote access options for third-party-secured devices are typically quite limited because users

cannot or should not install software onto them, and even advanced teleworkers cannot force most third-party devices to implement even rudimentary security precautions.

In today's computing environment, there are many threats to telework client devices. These threats are posed by people with different motivations, including causing mischief and disruption, and committing identity theft and other forms of fraud. The primary threat against most telework client devices is malware, including viruses, worms, malicious mobile code, Trojan horses, rootkits, and spyware. Malware threats can infect client devices through email, Websites, file-downloads and file sharing, peer-to-peer software, and instant messaging. The use of unauthorized removable media, such as flash drives, is an increasingly common transmission mechanism for malware. Another common threat is loss or theft of the device. Someone with physical access to a device has many options for attempting to view or copy the information. An attacker with physical access can also add malware that gives them access to data accessed from or entered into the device, such as users' passwords.

Permitting teleworkers to remotely access an organization's computing resources gives attackers additional opportunities to breach security. When a client device uses remote access, it is essentially an extension of the organization's own network. If the device is not secured properly, it poses additional risk not only to the information that the teleworker accesses, but also to the organization's other systems and networks. Therefore, telework client devices should be secured properly and maintained regularly.

Generally, telework client devices should have the same local security controls as other client devices in the enterprise – OS and application security updates applied promptly, unneeded services disabled, anti-malware software and a personal firewall enabled and kept up-to-date, etc. However, because of the threats that client devices face in external environments, additional security controls are recommended; some security controls may need to be adjusted to work effectively in telework environments. For example, storing sensitive data on a desktop computer housed at an organization's headquarters has different ramifications from storing the same data on a laptop used at several external locations.

Organizations should be responsible for securing their own telework client devices and should also require their users to implement and maintain appropriate, often similar, levels of security for personally-owned client devices. The mechanisms for securing organization-owned and personally-owned telework client devices are similar, but some of the security controls might not be feasible for teleworkers to implement on their own. See NIST SP 800-114, User's Guide to Securing External Devices for Telework and Remote Access, for recommendations for users securing their own telework client devices.

Other security measures particularly important for telework include the following:

Have a separate user account with limited privileges for each person using the telework PC. Teleworkers should use their limited privilege accounts for regular work and use a separate administrative account only for tasks that require administrator-level access, such as some software updates. This reduces the likelihood of an attacker gaining administrator-level access to the PC.

Enforce session locking, which prevents access to the PC after it has been idle for a period of time (such as 15 minutes) or permits the user to lock a session upon demand. After a session is locked, access to the PC can only be restored through authentication. Session locking is often part of screen-saver software. This prevents an attacker within physical proximity of a PC from easily gaining access to the current session. However, it does not thwart an attacker who steals a PC or has access to it for an extended period of time; session locking can be circumvented through various techniques.

Physically secure telework PCs by using cable locks or other deterrents to theft. This is most important for telework PCs in untrusted external environments, but is relevant for any environment, including home offices.

If teleworkers work from personal PCs, organizations might want to consider additional security controls. For example, some solutions provide a bootable OS on read-only removable media with pre-configured remote access client software. A user can insert this media into a PC and reboot the computer; this bypasses the PC's OS, which may be compromised, and loads the known-good OS and remote access client software from the removable media.

Another option is to provide teleworkers with specifically configured flash drives. These drives hold organization-approved applications that are executed from a read-only portion of the drives, which protects them from unauthorized modification. Temporary files are stored in another portion of the flash drives, which reduces the likelihood of data leakage onto the PC.

Securing Telework Consumer Devices

Many organization-controlled telework consumer devices can have their security managed centrally, at least to some degree. Organizations should take advantage of such security management capabilities whenever available, for example, by restricting the installation and use of third-party applications on cell phones and PDAs. However, many devices, including those not controlled by the organization, will need to be manually secured. Security capabilities and appropriate actions vary widely by device type and specific products, so organizations should

provide guidance to device administrators and users who are responsible for securing telework consumer devices.

NIST SP 800-124, Guidelines on Cell Phone and PDA Security, recommends safeguards for the most common types of telework consumer devices. The following are examples of these safeguards:

Limit the networking capabilities of consumer devices. This is particularly important for devices with multiple wireless capabilities; the teleworker might not even know that some wireless protocols are exposing the device to attackers. Even for devices with a single network connection, prevent users from inadvertently connecting the device to unintended host devices through technologies, such as Bluetooth and shared wireless networking.

For devices that face significant malware threats, run anti-malware programs. Devices that connect to the Internet may even have personal firewalls; these should be enabled to prevent attacks and unauthorized access.

Determine if the device manufacturer provides updates and patches. If so, ensure that they are applied promptly to protect the device from attacks.

Given the similarity between the functions of consumer devices, particularly as they become more advanced, and PCs, organizations should strongly consider treating them similar to, or the same as, PCs. This means that organizational policies for PCs may simply be extended to consumer devices; if the two policies are kept separate, the policy documents should heavily cross-reference each other.

Protecting Data

Telework usually involves creating and editing work-related information, such as email, word processing documents, and spreadsheets. Because that data is important, it should be treated like other important assets of the organization. Organizations can protect data by securing it on the telework device and periodically backing it up at a location controlled by the organization. Organizations can also choose not to allow the organization's information to be stored on telework devices, but, instead, to store it centrally at the agency.

Sensitive information, such as certain types of personally identifiable information (PII) (e.g., personnel records, medical records, financial records), that is stored on or sent to or from telework devices should also be protected. For example, teleworkers often forget that sensitive information on a zip drive used with their device, or printing the information on a public printer can also expose the information. An unauthorized release of sensitive or personal

information could damage the public's trust in an organization, jeopardize the organization's mission, or harm individuals.

Encrypting Data

All telework devices, regardless of their size or location, can be stolen. Some thieves may want to read the contents of the data on the device, and use it for criminal purposes. To prevent this, an organization should have a policy of encrypting all sensitive data when at rest on the device and on removable media. There are many methods for protecting data at rest, and they mostly depend on the type of device or removable media that is being protected. Some operating systems have their own data encryption mechanisms, and there are also numerous third-party applications that provide similar capabilities. See NIST SP 800-111, Guide to Storage Encryption Technologies for End User Devices, for more information on encrypting storage on client devices and removable media. Generally, when technologies, such as full disk encryption, are being used to protect data at rest, teleworkers should shut down their telework devices instead of placing them into sleep mode when they are finished with the work session. This helps ensure protection by the storage encryption technology.

Using Virtual Machines

If an organization has direct control over a telework device, the organization can enforce its policies for remote access, updating, etc. For other telework devices, such as PCs personally owned by teleworkers, the organization has a limited ability to enforce security policies. A method for controlling the teleworker's environment is to run a virtual machine (VM) on the telework PC. A user runs a VM image in the virtual machine environment; this image acts just like a full computer with an operating system and application software.

The organization distributes a VM image configured to be fully compliant with all relevant security policies. The teleworker then runs the VM image on the telework computer. When the image needs to be updated, the organization distributes a new image. Using a VM to support telework security works well, as long as the computer itself does not have any malware.

Organizations should consider encrypting all VM images used for telework to reduce the risk of compromise. This can be accomplished through the use of full disk encryption, file encryption, or other means. For high-risk situations, particularly involving access to highly sensitive information, organizations should encrypt each individual VM image used for telework and may also want to provide a second layer of protection through full disk encryption.

Backing-Up Data

Most organizations have policies for backing-up data on a regular basis. Such a backup policy should cover data on telework PCs and, if relevant and feasible, consumer devices. However, the policy may need different provisions for backups performed at the organization's facilities versus external locations. If the data to be backed-up contains sensitive or confidential information, additional security precautions must be taken, particularly at external locations.

If data is being backed-up remotely – from the telework device to a system at the organization – then the communications carrying that data should be encrypted and have their integrity verified. If data is being backed-up locally – to removable media, such as CD-R disks or USB flash drives, for example – the backup should be protected at least as well as the original data. For example, if the original data is encrypted, then the data in the backup also should be encrypted. If the original data is encrypted in a portable form, such as through virtual disk encryption or an encrypted VM image, then it may be sufficient to copy that encrypted entity onto the backup media. However, for non-portable forms of storage encryption, such as full disk encryption, the data would need to be decrypted on the telework device and then encrypted for storage on the backup media.

Key Practices for the Implementation of Successful Telework Programs

As agency telework coordinators develop, adapt, and expand their telework programs, seven key practices provide a basic framework for successful outcomes.

!
Must Do

- ☐ Planning
- ☐ Policy
- ☐ Performance management
- ☐ Managerial support
- ☐ Training and publicizing
- ☐ Technology
- ☐ Evaluation

Planning

Designate a telework coordinator

- ☐ Establish a cross-functional project team, including, for example, information technology (IT), union representatives and other stakeholders

☐ Establish measurable telework program goals

☐ Develop an implementation plan for the telework program

☐ Develop a business case for implementing a telework program

☐ Provide funding to meet the needs of the telework program

☐ Establish a pilot program

Policy

☐ Establish an agency-wide telework policy

☐ Establish eligibility criteria to ensure that teleworkers are selected on an equitable basis using criteria, such as suitability of tasks and employee performance

☐ Establish policies or requirements to facilitate communication among teleworkers, managers, and coworkers

☐ Develop a telework agreement for teleworkers and their managers

☐ Develop guidelines on workplace health and safety issues offsite

Performance Management

☐ Ensure that the same performance standards, derived from a modern, effective, credible, and validated performance system, are used to evaluate both teleworkers and office workers

☐ Establish guidelines to minimize adverse impact on office workers before work begins at alternate sites

Managerial Support

☐ Obtain support from top management for a telework program

☐ Address managerial resistance to telework

Training and Publicizing

☐ Train all involved, including, at a minimum, managers and teleworkers

☐ Inform workforce about the telework program

Technology

☐ Conduct assessment of teleworker and organization technology needs

☐ Develop guidelines regarding whether the organization or employee is to provide necessary technology, equipment, and supplies for telework

☐ Provide technical support for teleworkers

☐ Address access and security issues related to telework

☐ Establish standards for equipment in the telework environment

Evaluation

☐ Track participation numbers with a reliable system

☐ Collect data to evaluate the telework program

☐ Identify problems and/or issues with the telework program and make appropriate adjustments

Sustaining a Successful Telework Program

A Manager's Perspective

What's In It For Me?

☐ Compliance With The Mandate

As described in legislative background [Public Law number 106-346], telework should be implemented to the maximum extent possible.

☐ Human Capital Management Tool

Telework, like other flexibilities, can assist managers in attracting, recruiting, and retaining the best possible workforce. In addition, by decreasing employee commute times and other work/life stressors, telework can help make employees more effective in their jobs. Telework may also be used as a reasonable accommodation for disability.

☐ Emergency Response

Integrating work fully into an organization's operations and culture can help maintain critical functionality in the event of an emergency.

An Employee's Perspective

What's In It For Me?

☐ Work/life Balance

Telework gives employees more flexibility in meeting personal and professional responsibilities.

☐ Stress Reduction

Telework can help make life less stressful overall by reducing commuting time and adding to discretionary time.

☐ Freedom From Office Distractions

Offices can be busy places, especially in environments where employees work in cubicles. Distractions are plentiful. Many employees find they are able to focus and be more productive when they telework.

☐ Engagement

Employees who feel they have greater control over their work tend to feel more committed to their organizations.

The following is a sample of professions and job duties that typically can be considered for teleworking:

Accountant	Administrative Assistant	Engineer
Transcriptionist	Agent	Financial Analyst
Appraiser	Investigator	Word processing
Architect	Journalist	Web page design
Auditor	Lawyer	Writer
Budget Analyst	Manager	Engineer
Computer Scientist	Payroll transaction processing	Training Designer
Consultant	Programmer	
Contract Monitor	Psychologist	
Customer	Service Researcher	
Data Analysis	Scientist	
Data Entry Clerk	Systems Analyst	
Economist	Tax Examiner	
Employment Interviewer	Telephone-intensive tasks	

Remember Most "information-based" jobs are appropriate for teleworking. Teleworking is also ideal for jobs that require reading, writing, research, working with data and talking on the phone. Many jobs that may not seem appropriate at first may be modified so that the worker does the work most amenable to teleworking at home, one or two days a week.

Tips One of the secrets of designing a good telework program lies in the ability to organize specific jobs so that they can be done without constant interaction or need for feedback. Such delineation of tasks also increases

productivity because it makes use of the advantages of home and other work environments to achieve peak performance.

However, telework is NOT:

Work extension: many employees take work home with them. This is remote work, but it is not considered to be telework within the scope of the legislation.

Mobile work: some agencies have employees who, by the nature of their jobs, are generally offsite, and may even have their homes as "home base." Since the nature of their work requires this setup - usually, they are traveling much of the time - they are not considered to be teleworkers. This is different from "hoteling" arrangements, in which frequent teleworkers share space when onsite.

An employee right: federal law requires agencies to have telework programs, but does not give individual employees a legal right to telework.

Types of Telework Arrangements

The telework concept can be applied to a variety of alternative work environments. The work location might be:

☐ An employee's residence

☐ A telework center

☐ A traditional office or satellite office located closer to the employee's residence

☐ Another acceptable location, e.g., an office located in another state or country

The telework schedules can vary and are subject to management approval. They may be:

☐ Regular/recurring (for example, at least three days per week)

☐ One or two days a week

☐ Less than once a week, but at least once a month

In addition, telework may be a reasonable accommodation for people with disabilities.

Telework Centers

GSA, in cooperation with the Office of Personnel Management, is committed to providing telework as an available choice to both federal and private sector employees in the Washington, DC, area.

Working with community partners, GSA has established a network of 14 telework centers across the metropolitan area. These include:

Telework Centers
MARYLAND

Bowie State University Telecommuting Center
www.bowiestate.edu/telework (a nongovernment Website)
Bowie State University
14000 Jericho Park Road
Bowie, MD 20715
POC: Mi'Shaun Stevenson
Email: mstevenson@bowiestate.edu
(301) 860-4939
FAX (301) 352-4513

Frederick Telework Center
http://telework.ibacorp.us/ (a nongovernment Website)
7340 Executive Way, Suite M
Frederick, MD 21704
POC: Tonita Hickey
Email: hickeyt@ibacorp.us
(301) 698-2700 Ext. 101, FAX (301) 696-2848

Hagerstown Telework Center
www.hagerstowntelework.org (a nongovernment Website)
14 North Potomac Street, Suite 200a
Hagerstown, MD 21740
POC: Michael j. Pellegrino
(301) 745-5600 FAX (301) 766-2050

Prince Frederick Telework Center
www.teleworkctr.org. (a nongovernment Website)
205 Steeple Chase Drive #305
Prince Frederick, MD 20678
POC: Jill Wathen
Email: jillw@csmd.edu
(301) 934-7628 FAX (301) 934-7675

Waldorf Telework Center
www.teleworkctr.org. (a nongovernment Website)
128 Smallwood Village Shopping Center

Waldorf, MD 20602

POC: Jill Wathen

Email: jillw@csmd.edu

(301) 934-7628 FAX (301) 934-7675

Laurel Telework Center

(www.teleworkctr.org. a nongovernment Website)

13962 Baltimore Avenue

Laurel, MD 20707

POC: Jill Wathen

Email: jillw@csmd.edu

(301) 934-7628 FAX (301) 934-7675

VIRGINIA

City of Fairfax Telework Center at George Mason University

4031 University Drive, 1st floor

Fairfax, VA 22030

1st POC: Emeka Ezidinma – (703) 279-3301 / FAX (703) 359-9844

Email: eezidinm@gmu.edu

2nd POC: Keith Segerson – (703) 277-7724 / FAX (703) 277-7730

Email: segerson@gmu.edu

Herndon Telework Center at George Mason University

150 Elden Street

Herndon, VA 20170

1st POC: Emeka Ezidinma – (703) 279-3301 / FAX (703) 359-9844

Email: eezidinm@gmu.edu

2nd POC: Keith Segerson – (703) 277-7724 / FAX (703) 277-7730

Email: segerson@gmu.edu

Manassas Telework Center at George Mason University

10890 George Mason Circle

Bull Run Hall, Suite 147

Manassas, VA 20110

POC: Dr. Patricia Peacock, ppeacock@gmu.edu

(703) 993-9371 FAX (703) 993-8631

POC: Keith Segerson, segerson@gmu.edu

(703) 277-7724/ FAX (703) 277-7730

Fredericksburg (Formerly Spotsylvania)

www.gotelework.org (a nongovernment Website)

4956 Southpoint Parkway

Fredericksburg, VA 22407

POC: Peter Garcia, pgarcia@gotelework.org (540) 710-5001 FAX: (540) 710-5004

Stafford County Telework Center

www.gotelework.org (a nongovernment Website)

24 Onville Road, Suite 201

Stafford, VA 22556

POC: Keith Lesser, klesser@gotelework.org (540) 288-3000 FAX: (540) 288-3001

Woodbridge Telework Center

www.gotelework.org (a nongovernment Website)

13546 Minnieville Road

Woodbridge, VA 22192

POC: Tony Floyd, tfloyd@gotelework.org (703) 878-8500 FAX: (703) 878-8501

NetTech Center

www.nettechcenter.net (a nongovernment Website)

2281 Valley Avenue

Winchester, VA 22601

POC: Linda Whitmer

linda@nettechcenter.net

(540) 450-2222 FAX (540) 678-1939

WEST VIRGINIA

Jefferson County Telework Center @ BizTech

www.jctc.org (non-government Website)

150 E. Burr Boulevard

Kearneysville, WV 25430

POC: Beverly Bolger

bbolger@jctc.org

304.728.3051, x252 (o)   304.728.3068 (f)

Where Teleworkers Work

Teleworking away from the office

☐ Home

This is an in-home designated office space that meets company guidelines.

☐ Satellite office or telework center

Some employees enjoy using a telework center closer to their home than the company office. The space is owned or leased by one or more agencies, and may include approved centers established by state, local or county governments or private sector organizations.

☐ Hotels or airports

Many of these locations provide Internet access and are ideal for employees who travel often.

Teleworking in the office

☐ Desk sharing

Some employees may share offices and desks. One employee may work in the office on Mondays and Wednesdays, while another works on Tuesdays and Thursdays. The schedule can be formal or a flexible.

☐ Hot desking

Employees use the first available office space on a first-come, first-served basis. They can use passwords to access the company servers, and no single office area is dedicated for them specifically.

☐ Hoteling

Companies set aside empty office space designated for telework employees. Employees make reservations for the dates they need to use an office, and when they arrive the workspace is set up for them. At the end of the reserved time frame, teleworkers remove their belongings, and the space is ready for the next teleworker.

Virtual Teams

Teamwork is vital to many businesses, and understanding the various types of teams is important. They all have a parallel in the workplace and most already have a 'virtual' element. For example, an orchestra is a team of musicians. They meet to perform together a dozen or more times a year and practice and rehearse in sections (brass, violins, etc.). They play together in quartets or chamber ensembles, and also practice on their own. A teleworker is similar to the musician practicing on his or her own before rejoining one of the larger combinations when back in the office.

Remember

Virtual teams are a relatively new concept, but effective use of information and communication technologies can allow entire organizations to work at different locations, making companies more flexible and responsive. In many cases, the development of telework involves the creation and management of a virtual team. Some teams might train together but then work totally on their own for a shared objective.

Some teams, such as a traveling sales force, might meet only once or twice a year for a conference or team-building event and then spend the rest of their time working independently. Other teams may never meet, such as a consultant engineering firm building an

oil refinery. Designers can be located in Houston and Singapore, management in Perth and London, operational staff in Singapore and Delhi, and day-to-day management onsite outside Mumbai.

Individuals, including managers, sustain each of these teams. They demonstrate collective responsibility for shared objectives and understand their individual responsibilities. Each type of team also relies on organizational support.

Remember Another characteristic of successful teams, whether virtual or not, is the recognition that the team process is all about relationships. Such relationships are based on centralized information, streamlined knowledge transfer, and clear communication processes. Relationships also require employees' commitment in developing solutions.

Why virtual teams? Today's global environment, with its continued shift from production to service/knowledge increasingly places less emphasis on physical location. While there will always be a use for office workers and manufacturing facilities, many companies have turned to "outsourcing" work to individuals or groups. Tasks assigned to virtual teams range from the more routine, such as customer care, to highly specialized design or computer programming. The bottom line for creating a virtual team is that in order for the job to get done you don't need everybody physically there to do it.

Even as recently as the 1980s, office workers had a modicum of job security. However, in the current corporate climate, with its cost-cutting measures and mergers and acquisitions, no position is safe. Yet it is this very atmosphere that has fostered the proliferation of virtual teams. In creating these teams, management looks at such factors as organization-wide projects or initiatives; alliances with different organizations, some of which may be in other countries; and emerging markets in different geographic locations.

The fact that telecommuting has become increasingly popular with both companies and employees has also contributed to the development of virtual teams. Companies focused on the bottom line know it is cheaper to have someone on board who can do the job and who has the proper equipment and skills, no matter where they are based. Hiring a telecommuter can be cheaper than relocating a worker or paying for training or travel. For more information, see MASTERING VIRTUAL TEAMS, by Deborah Duarte and Nancy Tennant Snyder (San Francisco: John Wiley and Sons, 2006).

Supplement

Case Studies of Effective Telework Arrangements

Case Study I – State of North Carolina Teleworking Pilot Program and Lessons Learned.

The State of North Carolina committed to a one-year Teleworking Pilot Program. Its goal was to assess under what conditions a successful telework program could be implemented for state employees.

The objectives of the pilot were to:

* Develop, test and verify policies and procedures that could support a successful state teleworking program.

* Validate benefit expectations from telework as suggested by the State Auditor's report and teleworking programs in other states.

* Identify the problems/issues that could inhibit a telework program.

The Pilot Program attempted to answer the following questions:

* Policies: Can we create effective policies at the state level to support a successful telework program?

* Productivity: Can we measure productivity?

* Benefits: Can we quantify benefits and/or costs to the state?

* Issues: Can we identify issues and recommend solutions?

Pilot Background

The state auditor's report, "Establishing a Formal Telework/Telecommuting Program for State Employees," suggested that telework be considered as a management option that potentially could save millions of dollars:

We believe that increased use of telework (working from home) and telecommuting can offer the state benefits in terms of increased productivity of employees, avoidance of costs for office space, and decreased traffic congestion and pollution. The Governor, members of the Council of State, and the leadership of the General Assembly should work in concert to develop broad telecommuting policies that will allow state agencies to participate in the advantages of telecommuting.

The Office of State Personnel (OSP) was to develop policies and procedures to give guidance and consistency to an effective telework program and administer the State of North Carolina Pilot Teleworking Program. OSP assembled a cross-departmental, State Pilot Teleworking Advisory Committee, charged with developing and reviewing the progress of the State Telework Pilot Program. The committee had representation from policy areas and participating agencies. The Carolina Environmental Program at the University of North Carolina at Chapel Hill selected to develop, implement and evaluate the pilot program and make recommendations.

Pilot Participation

Five agencies participated in the pilot study: The Department of Environment and Natural Resources (DENR), Health and Human Services (DHHS), Administration (DOA), Insurance (DOI), and the North Carolina Community College System (NCCCS). There were a total of 64 teleworkers and 29 supervisors, nine of whom were teleworkers, as well. Twelve of these employees were hired directly into advertised telework/home-based positions. Additionally, 84 home-based employees and their 15

supervisors were added to the program. One agency had employees in Raleigh, as well as a regional office. The participation by agency is shown in Figure 1.

Participants in the pilot held a variety of jobs and came from a number of divisions. In DHHS, teleworkers came from Facilities Management and the Division of Child Protection. In DENR, participants were from Waste Management, Air Quality and a Regional Office. In NCCCS, participants were from the Auditing Division. In DOI, teleworkers came from Actuarial Services, Life and Health Division, Regulatory Actions and Financial Evaluation. In DOA, participants came from the State Property Office, Human Resource Management and the Agency for Public Telecommunications.

The time duration for teleworking extended from July through the following February. A majority of teleworkers began working from their homes by August-September, and completed six months or less of teleworking. While the limited participation and time span prohibited the use of conclusive productivity measurements, it did help highlight implementation issues.

Figure 1. Telework Participants

Agency	Teleworkers	Supervisors
DENR	36	16
DHHS**	13	2
NCCCS	4	2
DOA	4	2
DOI	7	7
Total	64	29
** 84 home-based employees also participated.		

Pilot Implementation and Lessons Learned

A "Lesson Learned" is an observation made during the pilot and written as a recommendation. It can serve as a flag for future planning efforts.

Senior Level Buy-in is Critical

No change can occur without buy-in from leadership. To be successful, teleworking must be embraced and promoted by senior management. All levels of management – senior, mid-level, direct line supervisors – as well as potential teleworkers must be informed. The primary communication channels used during the pilot were staff briefings, a teleworking Website, and email.

Tips

Lesson Learned - Since senior level buy-in is critical, the State Teleworking Program Coordinator should provide staff briefings. Senior level buy-in must be obtained and written communication to appropriate staff utilized.

Step One: Evaluation – Does Your Organization Need Teleworkers?

It was noted several times during the pilot that verbal commitments, such as "the Secretary is supportive" were not sufficient for lower-level managers to feel comfortable enough to pursue telework as a management option. As appropriate, division or other levels of management should also communicate their endorsement of teleworking.

Orientation Briefings

Orientation briefings were given to supervisors and potential teleworkers by the telework management or by a department representative. Most coordinators reported that scheduling orientation briefings was difficult.

Lesson Learned - A general orientation package should be created for use by anyone for staff briefing sessions. This will provide greater flexibility in scheduling.

Tips

Teleworking Website

The initial participants (first 75 teleworkers) in the pilot all reported that access to the Website was a good method for communication.

Lesson Learned - To improve the dissemination of information, several technologies should be integrated onto the telework Website. These include chat sessions, online surveys, online curriculum, group listserv, streaming video and database utilization.

Tips

Policies

Patterned after other state policies, a draft policy, "Teleworking Requirements for Pilot Programs," was formalized to establish interim guidelines for teleworking projects. With few changes, the telework pilot policy can be applied to establish a permanent program.

Lesson Learned - The state pilot teleworking policy was adequate for defining responsibilities and parameters for telework. As the pilot progressed, some questions arose concerning legal, public information, and health and safety issues. These issues might be best handled by state policy rather than departmental policies. Now that most departments have their policy in place, the state policy should be revisited to eliminate significant overlap. Coordinators requested to see other agency's policies as examples. This was not always possible since departments entered the pilot at varying times during the year. A coordinators' group should be convened to exchange ideas and to standardize a department level policy template as an aid to departments.

Tips

Teleworking Agreement

The last level of guidance was the Teleworking Agreement, a work contract between the supervisor and teleworker. Sample teleworking agreements were provided during training, completed, signed and placed in employee files.

Tips

Lesson Learned - The Telework Agreements should be reviewed by a human resource representative for consistency, adherence to policies, and for possible legal problems. In the pilot program, most department coordinators also happened to be human resource representatives, and they performed this function.

Coordinator Assignment and Duties

The Department Coordinator played a central role in the teleworking program, choosing projects, selecting personnel, and establishing policy. Training was provided for supervisors and teleworkers, but not for coordinators.

Tips

Lesson Learned - The coordinators are telework program directors for their respective agencies and would benefit by being familiar with multiple aspects of telework, including policies, human resource issues, technologies, finances, and public information to find solutions to questions and problems. Coordinators should be given a standardized handbook [or access to standardized online guidelines]. Each coordinator assembled his/her own information, including materials provided by the pilot program. Coordinators should have a standing committee that routinely meets to discuss issues, exchange ideas, and resolve problems.

Project Selection

Coordinators evaluated each supervisor, teleworker, and job for a match to a given set of known successful characteristics. This is standard practice in the teleworking community. The application process consisted of an online form submitted to the pilot manager and advisory committee by the coordinator.

Tips

Lesson Learned - Although the application process became a moot point for the pilot program, the acceptance criteria and procedure for evaluation should be implemented at the department level for future approval of telework projects. Department procedures should be developed by the coordinator and documented in the department policy.

Management Selection

A list of criteria for successful managers was presented to senior and mid-level managers and coordinators. Each department was given the ability to select its managers based upon the recommended characteristics. No formal process for supervisor selection was mandated.

Lesson Learned - A more rigorous process for selecting supervisors should be implemented at the department level. In some cases, supervisors were permitted to participate because they were "good managers," without regard to the skills required for managing a distributed workforce.

Tips

Teleworker Selection

All participating supervisors evaluated employees before approving their participation, using a set of characteristics required to effectively telework.

Lesson Learned - Proper screening of employees identifies good telework candidates and minimizes the risk of problems.

Tips

Results-oriented Management

Clear measurements of work results are the core of a successful telework program. Participants in the pilot program were asked to define work objectives in the application, in the employee and job screening process, and in the Telework Agreement. Supervisor feedback indicated three groups of management styles: 1) those that are, or are believed to be, already measuring objectively, 2) those that believe that some jobs cannot be evaluated with objective measures, and 3) those that believe measurement skills can be improved. All managers agreed that results-oriented management was a key element in successful teleworking.

Lesson Learned - Most managers participating in the program initially did not see a need and were reluctant to change their employee evaluation practices to accommodate teleworkers. Supervisors appreciated the need for results-oriented measures after teleworking began. Many adopted a more formal measurement scheme and also now apply it to office workers. Supervisory training in results management and measurement should be conducted and reinforced.

Tips

Training

Management training typically lasted between two-four hours. Emphasis was placed on management by results, screening qualified teleworkers, duties required, and related management issues.

Lesson Learned - Training for managers should be kept to a minimum, preferably no more than three hours. Most managers reported that extensive training was not required. It was suggested that follow-up training be provided online.

Tips

Managers would benefit from follow-up sessions to discuss in detail issues only highlighted during the training. Besides management by results, issues, such as peer employee impacts, turning down a telework applicant, administrative impacts, legal issues, and managing the distributed workforce, could be emphasized through Web-based training and a manager's online discussion group. Note. An impact is anything that has an effect, i.e., a peer employee impact might include a feeling of isolation by not being in physical contact with fellow workers, or feeling that promotion chances might be jeopardized by not being in the office. Administrative impacts could include increased productivity, decreased absenteeism, reduced parking space needs and increased employee retention.

Teleworker training covered many issues in a very short period of time. After teleworking for a few months, most teleworkers reported issues they recalled from training but required further information. The teleworkers indicated they would benefit from discussions with other teleworkers on how they handled similar issues.

Teleworkers without computers and Internet access stated they could benefit from training or information about technology use. In all cases, employees should be familiarized with virus protection and security, making backups, and effective use of the Internet and email. New coordinators should be given a thorough orientation to telework including the process for involvement and assessment, human resource issues, technology, finances and public information. They suggested that they could benefit from having a standing forum to exchange ideas and discuss issues.

Communicating For Success

Communication with supervisors, coworkers, and clients was the primary responsibility of the teleworker. In general, supervisors and teleworkers reported that they could use help with learning how to more effectively use email. Teleworkers, especially those who worked from home several days a week, reported feeling less a part of the organization. Supervisors, teleworkers, and coworkers need to communicate more effectively to maintain their group relationships.

Tips

Lesson Learned - Training on the development of Websites, instant messaging and other technologies, including whiteboards, would be useful for all participants.

Time Management

To a larger degree, the burden of time management shifts from the supervisor to the teleworker.

Lesson Learned - Most teleworkers reported a tendency to work more hours than required. This can result in employee burnout. Teleworkers can benefit from having guidance on the movement and management of information using today's advancing technologies. Teleworkers reported a change in their personal style of planning work to handle meetings, phone calls, and email more effectively. These changes should be captured and passed along to other teleworkers.

Tips

Safety and Security

Using a safety checklist, employees set up their offices without incurring additional expense. Pictures of the work site were requested to get a sense of what a typical office space would consist of and to identify any major ergonomic or safety concerns. No definitive guidelines were provided on confidentiality of materials other than the fact that they should be handled with care.

Lesson Learned - Ergonomic concerns and possible injuries due to extensive computer use at a desk may warrant the state assessing the value of providing furniture to teleworkers. In general, supervisors and teleworkers require more extensive information and guidance concerning safety and security issues.

Tips

Case Study 2 : Federal Judicial Center (FJC)

The Federal Judicial Center (FJC) is the research and training center for the federal courts, a function that puts a premium on effective communication and collaboration. According to Dr. Mark J. Maggio, FJC Education Division, "Our latest initiative is the Judicial Information Technology (JIT) project using WebEx technology to work with our judges' advisory committee in developing content and to help us train federal judges, who are busy people. The judges on our advisory committee have enthusiastically embraced this online training program. We can already point to a strong return on investment from the sheer ease of information delivery.

"JIT will also help to bring information technology into the judge's world. They can use it to help them in their day-to-day work, and we plan to teach them to use it remotely. We are also starting to train local IT staff so that they can take the training to judges hands-on. This is a significant initiative and it will be ongoing.

"Web-based communications expand our reach. We've traditionally performed face-to-face information transfer, but with tight budgets, we rely more and more on online communications. However, online work conferencing doesn't replace our current programs; it supplements and enhances them. Online conferencing gives us more flexibility.

"The nice thing about WebEx – which we've used for a few years – is that all you need is the Internet and the telephone, and you're all set. It's accessible to anyone we've attempted to reach. We use WebEx Meeting Center and Training Center to conduct everything from meetings to training to breakout groups."

Maggio pointed out that Web-based knowledge transfer is a powerful tool in the public sector, because government needs are constantly changing. Web-based conferencing doesn't just obviate the need to

purchase plane tickets or drive long distances – it makes meetings and presentations more robust, more compelling, and can accelerate processes and productivity.

WebEx technology also makes it possible for FJC to operate online, national workshops, which hundreds of people from around the country can attend remotely, without having to travel or take time from the office. WebEx's Training Center also promises to provide the agency with the ability to deliver more targeted educational and training content.

Telecommuting, he said, will only continue to grow. "Often, the more tailored the content is, the more engaging it is. This is allowing us to provide that higher level of engagement to our customers."

Case Study 3

Evaluation of the Work-at-Home Component of the Federal Flexible Workplace Pilot Project by the Flexiplace Management Team (FMT)

Flexiplace is a government-wide, nationwide project which allows federal employees to work at home or at geographically convenient satellite offices for part of the workweek. The FMT consisted of representatives of the General Services Administration, the Department of Agriculture, the Department of Justice, and the Office of Personnel Management.

The project consisted of three basic components:

* Work-at-home program

* Satellite work center program: This component involved the establishment of geographically convenient multi-agency satellite work centers which serve as alternate work sites for designated federal employees. Operating guidelines for satellite work centers are similar to those for work-at-home arrangements.

* Flexiplace accommodations for disabled workers: Participation in this component was available to disabled federal employees.

Supervisors submitted participant and control employee job performance ratings for three separate rating periods:

* (1) Baseline period (the six months before implementation of the pilot)

* (1) Baseline period (the six months immediately preceding

* (2) The first six months of the pilot

* (3) The final six months of the pilot

Supervisors submitted two types of job performance ratings: performance change ratings and performance level ratings. For the performance change ratings, supervisors indicated, for the given rating period, whether there had been improvement or decline in the participant's job performance relative to the participant's performance during the prior work year. Performance level ratings indicated the supervisor's perception of the level of job performance for a given rating period.

Summary of Participant Job Performance Ratings: More than 90 percent of the supervisors and 95 percent of the participants judged that Flexiplace job performance was either unchanged or improved relative to pre-Flexiplace performance levels. When considering the implications of "unchanged" job performance ratings, 84 percent of the participants entered the Flexiplace pilot with job performance

ratings of at least "exceeds fully successful" (44 percent with "exceeds fully successful" and 40 percent with "outstanding"). For the majority of the participants, therefore, Flexiplace job performance ratings of "unchanged" imply a very high level of performance.

Summary of Interpersonal Communications: The pattern of judgments regarding interpersonal communication is similar to that regarding job performance. More than 90 percent of the respondents, both participants and their supervisors, judged that there was no change in the effectiveness of work-related interpersonal communication; of those perceiving a change, significantly more saw an improvement as opposed to a decline in communication effectiveness.

Summary of Quality of Personal Life: Participants' responses indicate that Flexiplace has had a positive impact on their quality of personal life. More than half of the participants responded that there had been at least some improvement attributable to the advent of Flexiplace (only three percent or fewer reported a decline). This finding is particularly timely in view of the concern that American adults constantly feel pressed for time and feel that this time pressure has adverse implications for their families.

Summary of Quality of Work Life: Participant ratings of quality of work life were quite favorable, especially in view of the many personal and interpersonal adjustments involved. Regarding interpersonal relationship, job content, and most work environment factors, more than 90 percent of the ratings indicated no change or improved; a much greater proportion of the ratings indicated improvement as opposed to decline.

Summary of Participant Responses on Costs: More than 70 percent of the respondents reported reductions in job-related transportation and miscellaneous costs and no change in dependent care costs. Approximately one-third of the participants, however, experienced increased home maintenance costs due to participating in Flexiplace, probably due to an increase in utilities. In terms of overall cost assessment, more than half of the respondents indicated no change in job-related costs while nearly a third reported a reduction. That there was no change in dependent care costs appears to indicate that participants adhered to guidance that Flexiplace is not a direct substitute for child care.

Other Participant Responses: Participants indicated reductions in both sick leave and rush-hour vehicle usage. After one year in the project, 45 percent of the participants indicated that their Flexiplace sick-leave usage was generally lower, 82 percent indicated a reduction in rush hour usage of their private vehicles, while 35 percent indicated reduced non-rush hour vehicle usage. Less than six percent of the participants indicated increases in sick leave or vehicle usage.

Summary of Organizational Performance: Supervisory judgments on Flexiplace and organizational performance present a view of the collective functioning of participants and non-participants. The data suggest that Flexiplace is a feasible and desirable option for most organizations. More than 70 percent of the supervisors indicated that Flexiplace was feasible in terms of meeting organizational objectives and supervising participants and more than 90 percent indicated that Flexiplace did not result in significant organizational expenses. Finally, focus group summaries and information from agency Flexiplace coordinators suggest that some of the modifications desired by supervisors include more supervisor control over selection and number of participants, more guidance on technological issues, more flexibility in agency-specified procedures, and increased agency funding for the program.

Summary of Overall Reactions: The majority of the supervisors – 79 percent after six months, 80 percent after 12 months – and nearly all of the participants (99 percent after six months; 100 percent after 12 months) judged Flexiplace to be a desirable option requiring, at most, minimal refinement.

State Telework Best Practices

Commonwealth of Virginia

Virginia first studied telework in 1994 and subsequently passed legislation supporting a telework program in 2004. In 2006, Governor Tim Kaine signed Executive Order 35, strengthening the commonwealth's telework program by establishing the Office of Telework Promotion and Broadband Assistance in the Office of the Secretary of Technology. Virginia defined telework to mirror the standards used at the federal (and most local) levels. The commonwealth set a goal that 20 percent of its eligible workforce telework by 2010. In June 2008, Kaine announced an improved telework policy, directing all state agencies to consider ways to improve and expand agency telework and alternate work schedule programs.

Since its formation, the Office of Telework Promotion and Broadband Assistance has worked with the various branches of Virginia's government, including the governor's office, Department of Human Resource Management, Virginia Information Technology Agency (VITA), Department of Accounts (DOA), and Office of Commonwealth Preparedness to develop and institutionalize policies and procedures to increase the number of telework-eligible state employees. This is done not only because of the benefits telework provides, but also as a part of the continuity of government and pandemic preparedness planning process. The Office of Telework Promotion and Broadband Assistance worked with the legislature on five telework-related pieces of legislation and implemented several new telework-related policies, including those associated with the acceptable use of personal computers, security of commonwealth data, and payment of telework-related expenses.

Virginia state employees must telework one day per week, or 32 hours per month, to qualify as teleworkers. The commonwealth recently updated its data collection process and ultimately increased its number of eligible employees from 4,617 in 2007 to 22,764 in 2008, a huge leap. The number of active teleworkers in Virginia has steadily increased as well, growing from 2,712 as of September 2007 to 5,179 as of September 2008.

Virginia is unique in that it has both an inward facing telework initiative and an external program dedicated to increasing teleworking in the private sector – Telework! VA. Karen Jackson, director, Office of Telework Promotion and Broadband Assistance, outlined components that enable Virginia's effective telework program:

Strong policy framework: Agency leaders are more willing to initiate the process if decision-making and implementation are demystified; this reduces perceived risks.

Executive support: Governor Kaine's creation of the Office of Telework Promotion and Broadband Assistance, coupled with support from the Virginia Secretaries of Administration, Technology, Transportation, and Commerce and Trade, placed telework on the radar of agency heads, as well as commonwealth employees. The 2008 announcement of an executive branch telework initiative was a key endorsement as interest in the program continues to grow.

Team approach: Virginia has embraced the idea of a strong, collaborative team working to advance teleworking. Legislators, Governor Kaine and his cabinet and state agencies work to fill any gaps. Teamwork enables Virginia to move as quickly and effectively to develop and fully implement telework legislation and policies.

Serendipity: Like most governments these days, the commonwealth is looking to reduce costs. Telework is embraced as a creative solution for economic constraints, including budget, gas prices, traffic congestion, etc.

Telework technology solutions vary from agency to agency, but Jackson identified broadband as Virginia's key technology because of its critical role in a widespread telework initiative. She added that rising fuel costs have sparked an increase in teleconferencing and Web-based meetings – both of which require broadband in order to be effective. Beyond broadband, the commonwealth has benefited from effective policies that outline what is acceptable and ensure that agencies implement the best and most secure solutions.

State of Georgia

Georgia's state employee telework program was initiated by Executive Order in September 2003 as part of Governor Sonny Perdue's "Work Away" program. Perdue hoped that by establishing and promoting telework, the state would set a positive example for Georgia's private sector employers. He determined that telework would benefit Georgia in addressing major transportation, productivity, quality of life, employment, and environmental issues. Currently, Atlanta ranks among the top cities in traffic congestion, and the Environmental Protection Agency (EPA) has classified 28 counties in Georgia as non-attainment areas for ground-level ozone and/or particle pollution, resulting in poor air quality.

Perdue's Executive Order mandated that all departments and agencies seek opportunities to implement telework initiatives and alternate scheduling arrangements. It also created the position of a State Telework Coordinator, who coordinates, manages, and promotes the initiative and is a communication conduit for agencies and the public. Perdue also encouraged annual recognition for agencies for their participation. By June 2008, Georgia agencies reported 3,500 teleworkers.

Georgia's program, which was developed using a team from several agencies, is successful because of continuous support through the Governor's Office and other agency leadership. Training for managers and employees using the statewide telework policy has also been a critical component of Georgia's program, as well as the fact that Georgia incorporates a standard employee/employer agreement and promotes alternate workplace safety.

Dorothy Gordon, the State Telework Coordinator with Georgia's State Personnel Administration, said each agency determines its technology solutions based on the business needs of the organization. Georgia established its statewide policy on teleworking, as well as its Technology Security Guide to assist agencies in making their technology decisions. Metrics and state guidelines include:

- ☐ Surveys of both managers and employees
- ☐ Monthly reports for all Work Away Program areas showing:
  - ■ Number of teleworkers per agency
  - ■ Monthly commute miles saved are reported for combined Work Away program areas

Agencies and managers who may have been apprehensive about teleworking have been shown that, through proper management of the program, telework can be an effective business strategy. The positive effects of the initiative include increased employee productivity, enhanced employee morale and job satisfaction, commuter and environmental savings, and employee retention.

The state's telework program also helped lay the foundation for the passage of its Telework Tax Credit (Ga. Code 48-7-29.11). Georgia is the first state in the nation to offer employers a tax credit for teleworking. Businesses that pay State of Georgia income tax in 2009 are eligible for the tax credit.

Step Two: Selection – Putting Together a Teleworking Team

Successful Strategies for a Telework Program

☐ Create an advisory committee and appoint a telework coordinator

☐ Create telework guidelines for your managers and employees

☐ Create a telework agreement

☐ Determine start-up costs

☐ Plan how to implement the telework program

☐ Develop a training program

☐ Get final approval and prepare for implementation

☐ Implement and evaluate your program

!
Must Do

Create an Advisory Committee and Appoint a Telework Coordinator

An advisory committee should review your agency's telework policy and guidelines. A successful committee should be multidisciplinary, representing someone from every department and might include Human Resources, Legal, Facilities Management, Information Technology, Risk Management, an employee representative and/or a union representative. Of course, not all agencies have all of these departments, for example, in smaller organizations one person may do several jobs. Having representation from every department allows for a complete picture and is more likely to get buy-in from senior management. The group will also need a coordinator to oversee program development and implementation.

Create Telework Guidelines for Managers and Employees

These guidelines are the basis of your telework policy and will outline every component of the program. After implementation, use the guidelines as a checklist to ensure the program is running smoothly. Determining these guidelines is the most critical step on the success strategy checklist. The guidelines should also be customized to fit the needs of your agency.

Define the goals and benefits of your program

This will help avoid misunderstandings and encourage success.

In your organization's definition of teleworking, include both what it is and what it is not. Within this definition, explain the support provided for teleworkers, how much equipment is needed, and how much of it the company will provide.

- ☐ List your program's objectives.
- ☐ Describe the agency and employee benefits.
- ☐ These steps are the foundation of your telework plan.
- ☐ Determine what makes an employee eligible to telework

Guidelines should also provide an in-depth explanation of what determines eligibility, to ensure consistency in selection or non-selection of an individual to telework. It will prevent discrimination and protect your employees and agency. To determine what should make someone eligible to telework, consider the positions within your agency suitable for teleworking. Then, consider the employee traits associated with successful telework programs.

Some factors are:

- ☐ Employee performance
- ☐ Length of employment
- ☐ Each position's compatibility with teleworking
- ☐ Each employee's personality, suitability for teleworking, and role within the organization
- ☐ Also consider the traits of successful teleworker managers.
- ☐ Address technology and security issues

Determine the needed equipment and support for telework staff. Also, establish how you'll protect your agency's critical information. The more thoroughly you research these technologies, the more seamlessly the program will launch and run.

Technology usually plays a huge role in teleworking. And information access is one of the keys to a successful telework program. That's why it's vital to research the best ways to protect the teleworking program from a break in security. Of course, each organization's requirements are different. Determine what is right for your organization.

Determine the location of each telework employee

Employees need a work environment that promotes their productivity. So your organization will need to be certain that the offsite work environment is safe, and the

equipment is ergonomic. The company is liable for work-related accidents even when they occur in a home office. Taking this step will help you reduce liability risk.

☐ Determine if teleworkers will be working from home, another offsite location, or some combination of the two.

☐ Decide whether telework employees will also have an onsite office. One solution, "hoteling," allows employees to "check in" and be assigned to any available desk when they work onsite.

☐ Also, especially for home-based teleworkers, consider creating a checklist of workspace safety items.

Outline exactly what the agency expects from each teleworker

A successful telework plan outlines every aspect of your employees' responsibilities when working offsite. For example, telework guidelines might include:

☐ Specific times of the day or week for telework

☐ Methods employees use to contact designated managers or coworkers

☐ How employees should track their time

☐ How employees should care for dependents

☐ Tax implications of teleworking

☐ Circumstances that will cause an employee to lose telework privileges

☐ Align telework policies with any existing organizational policies

---

Once you've completed your telework policy, review it against other organizational policies. If it has a major impact on existing policies, something may need to be adjusted. But also consider how large the change is, and whether it is needed to address teleworking. If it helps to increase productivity, perhaps it is allowable. Consistency is the overall goal.

Remember

Determining Telework Arrangements

When setting up telework arrangements for staff, always develop a Telework Agreement. Different agencies may have different requirements: check with your telework coordinator for a sample agreement that can be used as a template.

To determine appropriate telework arrangements, consider the employees' work habits and the suitability of their assigned tasks. Selecting employees and tasks right for telework is a key factor in successful management. Both elements are important: the tasks must be suited to being done offsite, and the person must have the skills and predisposition to work successfully

while working remotely, with their prior performance record indicating likely success in telework.

Determine tasks suitable for telework by focusing on the nature of the work rather than on job title, type of appointment, or work schedule. Begin with the assumption that all positions include at least some tasks that may be suitable for telework. This approach will extend telework to the widest range possible of employees.

To head off many preventable problems, agreements should clarify the terms of the arrangement and the responsibilities of both parties before telework begins.

Some typical examples include:

☐ The telework time schedule (i.e., days and hours)

☐ The telework site

☐ What technology is needed to do the work

☐ What equipment/materials/services the agency will provide and what will be the employees' responsibility

☐ How technology requirements will be handled (e.g., set up and maintenance)

Remember Keep in mind that the Telework Agreements between you and your employees do not have to be formal. Telework Agreements can be oral and confirmed through a casual letter or email. But something always must be written down and then filed for protection of both teleworker and manager.

Additionally, Telework Agreements:

☐ Can be time-limited for a trial basis

☐ Can, and generally should, be tailored to the individual, even if you have multiple teleworkers in the same job; two people in the same job don't necessarily have the same responsibilities, the same tenure, or the same skills

☐ Can be canceled if things are not working out with an employee; such cancellations should be conducted with proper notice to the teleworker, in accordance with agency procedures, and after reasonable attempts to resolve the issues

☐ Can be modified from time to time to accommodate new requirements/circumstances; you may want to review the agreement periodically and fine-tune it based on actual experience

Note: Very few jobs are suited in their entirety to telework; what you're looking for are the parts of the job that can be done as well or better remotely. Depending upon their duties, the worker could be out of the office from three to four days a month to the same amount of days per week. With your guidance, employees wanting to telework should be able to separate the tasks, if any, that must be done in the office from those that can be accomplished remotely.

Tips

Create a Telework Agreement

A Telework Agreement is the specific form that each teleworker and manager fills out, agrees to, and signs. This agreement defines mutual expectations on every aspect of the job, including communication and feedback. The agreement can also be used by managers to evaluate the teleworker. While the telework policy contains general information about the program, the telework agreement has specific details about each position. No matter how frequently or rarely an employee teleworks, a written agreement should be executed between the employee and manager. The agreement should include:

☐ The teleworker's offsite location and contact information

☐ Teleworking start and end dates

☐ A list of supplies and equipment provided by the agency

☐ Tasks to be performed while teleworking

☐ Expectations for communicating

☐ Safety checklist

☐ Expectations for emergency telework

You may want to leave room for flexibility. For example, you may not yet want to write down the exact days the employee will work on or offsite. Instead, specify that the telework schedule will be determined on a weekly basis, depending upon work responsibilities.

Tips

The agreement should also contain a statement indicating that the employee has read and agrees to the agency's telework policy and safety guidelines. Both the teleworker and his or her manager should review and sign the form. Other signatures may be required, such as a member of the IT department responsible for providing the equipment. Telework Agreements need to be updated as circumstances change (e.g., if the telework schedule changes). The manager and teleworker should work together to evaluate the arrangement periodically, make changes in the agreement as necessary, and re-sign the document. In the first year, this may happen within a few months; thereafter, perhaps annually.

Safeguard Information and Data

! Must Do You must ensure that employees realize that they are responsibility for the security of the data and other information they handle while teleworking. Employees should:

Be familiar with, understand, and comply with their agency's information security policies

Participate in agency information security training

Maintain security of any relevant materials, including files, correspondence, and equipment, in addition to following security protocols for remote connectivity; depending on the sensitivity of the information being handled, the home office may need to include security measures, such as locked file cabinets, similar to what may be used in the work site

Costs

Long-term increases in productivity and other goals should be factored into start-up costs. The cost-saving benefits of teleworking will most likely repay your initial investment, and continue to save the agency money. Following are three groups of expenses to consider:

1. Software, security, files, and computer and telecommunications equipment needed for remote offices; also consider the costs for transporting, installing, maintaining and insuring this equipment for loss

2. Additional telework training expenses, including training for new teleworking equipment and software, working remotely, or supervising teleworkers

3. Miscellaneous costs associated with setting up your program, including manager's and worker's time, technical support, designing the budget, and human resource policies

Many organizations find the set-up expenses absorb quickly through cost savings once the program is implemented. As you add up the start-up costs of your telework program, remember the long-term benefits the program will provide. Cost savings and productivity increases will most likely repay your initial investment, and continue to save more money in the future.

Determine Start-Up Costs

Costs associated with a telework program start-up will vary according to organizational goals and objectives. Assessing your organization's existing technology and equipment will help determine your initial start-up expenditures. The following items should be considered:

Computer equipment - Is it employer issued, or will employees need to provide their own equipment?

Accessory equipment - Will an employee need a phone, printer, fax machine, Webcam, scanner, etc., to complete work tasks?

Information Technology - Software, email system, server needs, security precautions, etc.

Training - While some free training is available online, a company may want to invest in onsite training for employees and managers.

Labor associated with program set-up - Systems should be configured to ensure that telework is seamless for both internal and external customers. There should also be a review of computer/software requirements, notification to participants/ employees, HR revisions to employee manuals, and development of policy and procedures associated with the telework program.

Savings and Other Benefits

Like costs, these will vary, and may include:

Real estate costs - Preventing the increased rent that accompanies a need for more space, or reducing a company's rent by decreasing its need for space

Overhead costs related to office space, equipment

Increased productivity will impact the need to hire additional employees

Lower employee turnover

Increased morale may result in heightened productivity levels

Cost Analysis

The General Services Administration (GSA) commissioned the Telework Technology Cost Study to investigate potential cost impacts to federal agencies of information technology (IT) infrastructure expansion to accommodate increased home-based telework, identify technologies needed to support widespread telework deployment, and provide guidance to federal organizations in justifying IT infrastructure expansion to support their telework programs. The study found that federal organizations already have some elements of IT infrastructure to support limited levels of telework, but lack strategies for IT support of widespread telework, including telework considerations in agency investment planning

or technology enhancement initiatives. Although closing the gap and providing a robust telework infrastructure will require careful planning and investment of agency resources, the potential benefits are far-reaching and cost beneficial. Appropriate top level support, program management, capital planning, coordination with other agency initiatives, and full consideration of telework value will result in infrastructure improvements, which will provide full realization of agency IT investments. Cost must be considered, and this study provided information needed to support infrastructure improvement initiatives.

Plan How to Implement the Telework Program

Many agencies choose to start with a pilot program, which is an excellent way to test whether teleworking is viable. Launching a smaller-scale, trial program can have the following benefits:

It allows you to commit at your comfort level.

It provides a controlled environment for setting employee-management expectations.

It provides time to evaluate program effectiveness and make adjustments.

It offers a built-in exit strategy, should you decide against teleworking.

Develop a Training Program

Tips

Training is beneficial for anyone who interacts with teleworkers and will ensure a smoother launch.

Teleworking training should be designed for:

☐ Teleworkers

☐ Managers of teleworkers

☐ Any onsite employees interacting with teleworkers; these employees will learn effective ways of communicating with those offsite

☐ Your IT or technology division; most likely, your teleworkers will rely on technology and should be trained by IT staff on technology policies, including how to access company servers, email, etc.

This is only the initial training, and new managers and teleworkers will also need training.

Step Two: Selection – Putting Together a Teleworking Team

Get Final Approval and Prepare For Implementation

Once the telework program is outlined and receives approval from upper management, it is ready to be launched. This involves the following:

Remember

- ☐ Announce your telework program to staff, ask interested employees to submit their applications, and select your telework pilot program staff.
- ☐ Purchase or lease equipment and software if necessary.
- ☐ Collect signed telework agreements.
- ☐ Train selected employees.
- ☐ Set the program start date.
- ☐ Administer a pre-telework evaluation to use later as a follow-up survey.

Implement and Evaluate Your Program

After six months or so, evaluate your program and then determinate regular intervals for periodic re-evaluation. An evaluation program can measure the progression and value of the program and identify areas needing adjustment. Then compare the results to your pre-telework or earlier telework evaluation and make improvements where needed. Measure and compare:

Remember

The performance of teleworkers, telemanagers, and non-teleworking colleagues

- ☐ Productivity
- ☐ Costs
- ☐ Recruitment
- ☐ Retention

Success Factors for Effective Telework

The more you know about telework the better prepared you will be to develop a successful telework arrangement. You must constantly review your agency's telework policy so that you fully understand the telework procedures and guidelines, and you should contact your agency's telework coordinator if there is anything you do not understand. When managers and employees openly support the telework program, you know it is successful. Visit http://www.telework.gov/ for additional information about the federal government-wide telework initiative.

Must Do

Other measures to ensure success:

☐ Define the details of the telework arrangement early, and revisit them as often as needed.

☐ Depending on agency policy, the actual agreement might take the form of:

☐ An oral agreement, in the case of situational or episodic telework

☐ An email to an employee confirming the agreement

☐ A formal written agreement

☐ Ongoing and effective communication among all stakeholders is a priority for everyone.

While effective communication is a key ingredient in any work setting, it is especially important in telework. Make the effort to ensure effective communication – up, down and across – through emails, telephone/conference calls, and face-to-face meetings. For teleworkers, the amount of communication required may depend on the nature of the work and the amount of time you are teleworking. For example, if you only telework one day per week to keep up with correspondence, it may be sufficient that your manager and coworkers are able to reach you, if needed, on telework days. If you are teleworking several days a week, you may need to do more to ensure adequate contact. If you are a senior manager you, or a deputy, should be available at all times. Listed below are some areas for teleworkers to consider:

Receiving phone calls (if required)

☐ You may have your incoming phone calls forwarded to your telework site or you may need to check voicemail on a regular schedule and respond accordingly.

☐ Sending and receiving email

☐ You should be able to send and receive email as if you were in the office.

☐ Conference phone calls (if required)

You should be able to conduct or participate in conference phone calls from your telework site.

☐ Accessing work collaboration tools and programs

☐ You should be able to login to your local network from your telework site to retrieve files, access programs, and share schedules.

Remember

Establishing Communication Procedures

Key to succeeding as a manager of teleworkers is communicating effectively with your staff. Some staff members need, and benefit from, a daily check-in to review what they are doing or have done, what their

next task is, and what problems they might be experiencing. Other teleworkers may require less frequent contact with the manager but instead need to collaborate regularly with coworkers. When establishing communication guidelines with your teleworking employees, determine:

- What needs to be communicated?

- Who needs to communicate with whom (e.g., manager, customers, coworkers)?

- How the teleworker will communicate (e.g., when email is sufficient or a phone call is warranted)?

Three criteria determine the best communication methods.

Predictable access is more important than instant access in most cases. You probably don't need to reach your teleworkers immediately all the time – even this can't always be accomplished in the office – but you do need to agree when you will be able to reach them, or at least hear back from them if you leave voicemail or email.

Tips

Try to adopt a "no hassles, no surprises" approach for coworker and customer contacts. Your teleworkers should be reachable in roughly the same ways and with the same responsiveness when working out of the office as in. For example, use the same phone number and return calls should be received within the same interval.

Pick the right tools for the right times and right places. You and your teleworkers have a full communications toolkit - voice, voicemail, in-person meetings, email, fax, conference calls, and more. Use each one only for the things it does best, e.g., don't use voicemail to leave a long message with a series of complex budget figures that would be sent better by fax or email, and don't try to conduct visually-oriented training or problem-solving sessions over an audio conference line.

Most managers of teleworkers learn quite quickly that many issues that would seem to justify immediate access or an interruption in the office can actually wait until, for example, the next time you talk on the phone or see the teleworker. Not everything that seems urgent actually is; something is critical only if there is a consequence to delaying it. If waiting an hour, or even a day, won't create problems, then don't create an interruption for an otherwise highly productive teleworker.

Tips

Make sure the appropriate technology is available. Managers and teleworkers should determine what equipment is needed to telework effectively and meet performance expectations. The agency telework policy may dictate this; specifying available office equipment and technology support. It may also set forth what teleworkers must provide for themselves.

Take steps to ensure that telework works for customers, coworkers, and other key staff. A telework arrangement is only successful if it works for everyone involved, not just the teleworker. Discuss and determine appropriate and effective practices for working with coworkers, as well as customers and other key agency staff. Plan for the following:

☐ Make sure customers' needs come first.

☐ If applicable, plan office work days around customers' needs.

☐ Have incoming phone calls forwarded to the telework site.

☐ Check voicemail on a regular schedule, and respond as you would if you were in the office.

☐ Send and receive email as if you were in the office.

☐ Conduct or participate in conference phone calls from your telework site.

Remember Ensure there is mutual trust among manager, teleworkers and coworkers. The key difference between the telework relationship and the in-office relationship is that managers cannot see what teleworkers are doing. Are they working or walking the dog? Are they performing their duties or chatting on the phone with friends? It all comes down to trust.

As a manager, you will know you can trust your teleworkers when they complete assignments on time, pitch in to help when the pressure is on, offer new ideas, volunteer for projects, work independently without the need for close supervision, and keep you informed about what they are working on and what they have accomplished.

Expect a trial period, during which you will meet frequently to discuss how things are going. Does the schedule work for everyone? Is the quality and quantity of telework up to your expectations? Do the specifics in the agreement need to be changed? These discussions may become less frequent as your confidence in the ability to manage the telework grows. However, some discussions will always be part of your managerial routine communication and performance assessments.

Remember Managers must ensure that they hold everyone to the same standards. You must be open and public and not show any special favors. It is also important to maintain your non-working relationships as appropriate, with your teleworkers.

Common Employee Concerns Regarding Telework

It might jeopardize my chances for promotion.

While this should not be a concern, the old adage, "out of sight, out of mind" causes some teleworkers to worry, especially those who telework full-time. If advancement is based on performance and managers are evaluating every employee's performance by the same standards, it should not matter whether one teleworks or works in the office. However, teleworking is a new system for many managers, and they are adjusting to it. You can help yourself and your manager by maintaining a high level of communication. Provide regular updates on your work. Keep track of your accomplishments and review them with your manager during your performance appraisal. Pass along positive feedback from customers. Your objective is to make sure your manager is aware of the quality of your work and your commitment to the organization.

Remember that it is your responsibility to keep track of opportunities for advancement and to make sure your manager knows of your interest in taking on more responsibility. Stay in contact with your

colleagues in other offices to learn of new job openings. Prospective employers will probably view your telework experience positively. It demonstrates your ability to work independently and to organize your time effectively.

I may not like working alone.

While some employees may not be comfortable working alone, with the advances in technology, teleworkers are no more isolated than workers in an office setting. They can communicate readily by telephone, email, Instant Messaging, and texting, delivering and receiving information through fax and file transfer. To some extent, teleworkers, office workers, and managers can communicate and keep in touch through social media, such as Twitter or Facebook. Although these are primarily social networking sites, they are also used in a somewhat professional context, similar to stopping by the local pub, restaurant or sports bar for "happy hour" with coworkers.

Teleworkers can also participate in meetings via conference calls. Without the sometimes annoying and disruptive cubicle drop-ins, they can have all the contact they want and still have the quiet time to focus on a task when needed.

Can I live up to my manager's expectations?

Some employees are so eager to telework that they are willing to promise anything for the chance to work from home. Once they start teleworking, they realize they created some unrealistic expectations for their manager. They feel guilty if performance slips, and their manager feels let down. The best way to meet employers' expectations is to create reasonable ones and then be dedicated in living up to them.

Will I be able to separate home and work?

There are two parts to this question: the physical aspect and the emotional aspect. Physically, teleworkers need to identify a space for equipment and working environment. Is there enough room to do the work? Is it quiet? Can they talk on the phone without disturbing anyone? Many people are not sure whether they can block out distractions until they try it. Some people find it very difficult to do. They may need the structure the office setting provides.

Necessary Skills

Successful teleworkers need work habits that support independent task performance. These may include:

!
Must Do

- ☐ The ability to work with minimal direct supervision
- ☐ Organized work practices
- ☐ Productive work skills
- ☐ Good planning skills
- ☐ The ability to meet schedules and deadlines
- ☐ Effective time management skills
- ☐ Effective communication
- ☐ Ability to handle work tools (computers, email, printers, etc.) independently

These work habits help in any job, but are particularly important for successful telework.

Overcoming Barriers to Telework

Sometimes the greatest resistance to telecommuting can come from the managers. They not only may feel threatened by a new idea and different methods of working, they may also feel they are losing control by allowing people to do their tasks offsite. Much of this depends on the managers' orientation; if they are used to walking around and physically supervising workers, how can they do this remotely without feeling nonessential or that their own jobs might be in jeopardy? Experts agree that management cooperation with telecommuting can make or break the program.

Tips

Thus, the evaluation committee should determine whether the current management style is compatible with the proposed telecommuting arrangement. The managers' flexibility and level of trust, as well as their communications skills, would be factors to consider. One solution may be retraining managers in how to supervise teleworkers. "They must move from monitoring attendance to managing performance," observe "Effects of Telecommuting Organisational Behaviour" authors Margaret Tan-Solano and Professor Brian H. Kleiner. In other words, they need to be results-oriented instead of task or time oriented, not an easy change if managers are accustomed to working in a certain way.

For example, Michael Amigoni, former Chief Operating Officer for ARO, Inc., a leading outsourcing provider of offsite remote call center agents and skilled back-office professionals, encountered resistance from some of the more traditional managers during the early days when ARO was switching to remote workers. After identifying them, he attempted to work with them in learning how to revise their management style to a more results-focused orientation. Most were amenable to change and, although they may have been uncomfortable initially, eventually they came around to the new way of working. The one exception was let go fairly early during the switchover, so as not to undermine its effectiveness and success.

Workshops need to cover everything from new logistics and technologies to revised team and organizational protocols to different methods of evaluating and rewarding performance. For instance, since they can't holler over the cubicle or stop by for a chat, managers may need to brush up on their telephone and email skills.

At least part of the program should consist of "team training" in which the telecommuter and manager come together. "The telecommuter has to understand what the supervisor's problems are going to be and vice versa," points out author George Piskurich. These joint sessions can include negotiating and planning basic issues, such as hours the employee will be available and when and how often he will communicate with the manager.

It is likely that you will have to make some adjustments as a manager in how you do business to accommodate telework.

Tips

Work Planning/Scheduling Requirements

When you are in the office every day, an impromptu meeting is not a problem. If you have part-time or full-time teleworkers, however, you need to plan meetings in advance or be available. When handing out work assignments, you may need to coordinate schedules. Be flexible to accommodate your teleworker's scheduling requirements.

Effective work planning can support team efforts across time and space. Just as with working in the office, managers, teleworkers and office workers need to establish guidelines for working in a team environment.

Workflow Process Changes

If your office work processes are entirely paper-based, you may need to explore electronic alternatives, which may be more efficient and cost-effective. For example, several agencies are replacing their manual correspondence control processes with automated systems for document review, revisions, and approval. These automated systems allow teleworkers to participate fully in essential business processes.

Changes in Manager/Employee Relationships

Your management style may involve walking around to casually check on progress on an assignment. You may also maintain an "open door policy" for staff to ask questions and raise concerns.

As a manager, you'll need to figure out how to monitor the progress of employees, while maintaining access to all coworkers, whether home or office-based. These mechanisms should be detailed in the telework agreement. There may be more "e-walking around" or managing over the phone or via email.

Information Security Issues

Teleworkers must take responsibility for the security of the data and other information. This means they should:

Be familiar with, understand, and comply with their agency's information security policies

Participate in agency information security training

In addition to following security protocols for remote connectivity, maintain security of any relevant materials, including files, correspondence, and equipment; depending on the sensitivity of the information being handled, the home office may need to include security measures, such as locked file cabinets, similar to those used in the work site

Technology

The final challenge to a successful telework program involves information and communication technology. Full-time teleworkers will likely require a more technologically equipped office set-up than someone who only teleworks occasionally. Two issues that need to be clarified are initial installation of the equipment and ongoing monthly costs to maintain the services. The telework agreement should specify who pays for what, based on agency policy.

Characteristics of Effective Teleworkers

Conduct an Honest Self-Assessment

A successful telework arrangement starts with a good self-assessment. Employees should consider the following factors in making an honest determination about their telework capabilities:

- ☐ Sufficient portable work for the amount of telework being proposed
- ☐ Ability to work independently, without close supervision
- ☐ Comfort with the technologies needed to telework
- ☐ Good communication with manager, coworkers, and customers that will enable a relatively seamless transition from onsite to offsite
- ☐ Telework office space conducive to getting the work done
- ☐ Dependent care (i.e., child care, elder care, or care of any other dependent adults) arrangements in place
- ☐ Ability to be flexible about the telework arrangement to respond to the needs of the manager, the workgroup, and the workload

Plan the Work

Employees who telework should assess the portability of their work and the level of technology available at the remote location. They will need to plan their telework days to be as productive as possible by considering the following questions:

- ☐ What files, documents, and equipment will I need to take when I leave my regular workplace the day before teleworking?

☐ Who needs to be notified that I will be teleworking?

☐ What other steps should I take before leaving the office (e.g., forwarding the phone)?

☐ In the case of emergency telework, what should I have available at all times at my home office or, if applicable, a telework center, to enable me to be functional without coming onsite to retrieve materials?

Manage Expectations and Communication

Managers are ultimately responsible for the effective functioning of the workgroup. Nevertheless, to avoid any negative impact from their arrangement, teleworkers should help manage the group's expectations and their own communication. Issues that should be addressed include the following:

Backup: Even with very portable work there are inevitably instances where physical presence is required and a coworker may need to step in. Coworker backup should be planned, reasonable, and reciprocal. Cross-training of staff has broad organizational benefits and should be a management priority.

On-the-spot assistance: Teleworkers may occasionally need someone who is physically in the main office to assist them (e.g., to fax a document or look up information). Again, these arrangements should not be unduly burdensome; a "buddy system" between teleworkers may be the most feasible solution. For example, if one teleworker needs a document or piece of office equipment, he or she can contact another teleworker (or the manager) who is in the office that day and arrange for a pickup at a mutually convenient location. The favor will be reciprocated as needed.

Communication with manager: The manager must be kept apprised of the teleworker's schedule, how to make contact with the teleworker, and the status of all pending work.

Communication with coworkers: Coworkers must be informed about the appropriate handling of the teleworker's telephone calls or other communications.

The Bottom Line

Teleworkers MUST—

Comply with the security and telework policies of their agency

Take responsibility for ensuring the success of their arrangement

Notify the manager of any changes in their situation that may affect the arrangement

Teleworkers MAY NOT—

No No Assume a telework arrangement is permanent

Use telework as a substitute for child or other dependent care

Teleworkers MAY—

Use appropriate grievance procedures if they believe their telework request or agreement was wrongfully denied or terminated; telework requests or agreements may be denied or terminated only for business reasons, and managers must provide written justification to the affected employee.

Basics for Managers

To comply with the legislation, managers must be committed to using telework to the fullest extent possible. Beyond the basic requirements outlined above, managerial skill, participation, and support can make telework a real asset to an organization.

These basic steps will help minimize any potential administrative burden, maximize the benefit of telework for you and your workgroup, and set the stage for employees to be successful, whether or not they are teleworking.

Know Your Telework Coordinator

Each agency must designate a telework coordinator who acts as a key contact for policy and program questions. Managers should maintain frequent contact with their telework coordinator to ensure the agency's policy and procedures are properly applied and that the coordinator is aware of the full range of available support and resources.

Know Your Policy and Procedures

As detailed in §359 of Public Law 106-346, all agencies must have a telework policy. Managers should familiarize themselves and their employees with their agency policy to ensure they are in compliance with its requirements.

In addition, all agencies should have policies on information systems and technology security, and managers must ensure their equipment choices and telework agreements comply with this policy. Information security includes protection of sensitive "hard-copy" files and documents.

Participate in Training

Online telework training for managers is available [http://www.telework.gov/Tools_and_Resources/Training/Managers/index.aspx]. In addition, many agencies offer telework training, and telework coordinators are available to consult with managers.

Information technology security training, administered at the agency level, is mandatory, and managers should ensure that teleworkers complete these programs and understand their responsibilities in safeguarding work-related information.

Determine Employee Eligibility

Generally, agencies have discretion to determine telework eligibility criteria for their employees. These criteria should be detailed in agency policy. Individual managers should assess who is/is not eligible in their workgroup based on eligibility guidelines and any applicable collective bargaining agreements. Some agencies may provide managers additional discretion in deciding whether to grant or deny a request to telework from an eligible employee, based on additional factors, such as staffing or budget.

All employees are considered eligible for telework except the following:

Remember

Employees whose positions require, on a daily basis (i.e., every work day), direct handling of secure materials or onsite activity that cannot be handled remotely or at an alternative work site, such as face-to-face personal contact in some medical, counseling, or similar services; hands-on contact with machinery, equipment, vehicles, etc., or other physical presence/site dependent activity, such as forest ranger or guard duty tasks..

Employees whose last performance rating of record (or its equivalent) is below "Fully Successful" (or the agency's equivalent) or whose conduct has resulted in disciplinary action within the last year. (Agencies may require a rating of record higher than "Fully Successful" for eligibility, but must still report all employees rated "Fully successful" or higher as eligible.)

Understand and Assess the Needs of the Workgroup

Telework is often implemented on a case-by-case basis, rather than strategically, as individuals request arrangements. This reactive approach carries the risk of raising fairness issues, with decisions about telework arrangements being made on a first-come, first-served basis. Telework should be implemented strategically, taking into account the needs and work of the group, rather than granting or denying requests one by one. Employees

should participate in the process and may be asked to help formulate possible solutions and suggestions for equitable and fair telework.

Create Signed Agreements

Tips

The manager should enter into a written agreement with his or her teleworker for every type of telework, whether the employee teleworks regularly or not. The parameters of this agreement are most often laid out by the agency policy and/or collective bargaining agreement, but should include certain key elements:

- ☐ Location of the telework office (e.g., home, telework center, other)
- ☐ Equipment inventory - what employee is supplying, what agency is providing, and if applicable, what the telework center is providing
- ☐ In general, the job tasks that will be performed while teleworking
- ☐ Telework schedule
- ☐ Telework contact information (e.g., what phone number to use on the telework day)
- ☐ Safety checklist certifying that the home office meets certain standards

Expectations for emergency telework; specify whether the employee is expected to telework in the case of a Continuity of Operations (COOP) event, pandemic, weather shutdown, other unusual local conditions that may substantially affect commuting, etc.

Most importantly, the agreement should be signed and dated by the manager. Managers should keep copies of all telework agreements on file.

Telework agreements are living documents and should be revisited by the manager and teleworker and re-signed regularly, preferably at least once a year. At a minimum, new telework agreements should be executed when a new employee/manager relationship is established.

OPM strongly recommends that any individuals asked to telework in the case of a COOP event or a pandemic health crisis have a telework agreement in place that provides for such an occurrence. Such individuals also should practice teleworking on a regular basis as much as possible.

Communicate Expectations

The telework agreement provides a framework for a discussion about expectations between the manager and the employee. This discussion regarding both routine and emergency telework will help clarify basic issues, such as the following:

How will the manager know the teleworking employee is on or off duty? (Signing in, signing off procedures may be needed.)

How will the manager know the work is being accomplished?

What technologies will be used to maintain contact?

What equipment is the agency providing? What equipment is the teleworker providing?

Who provides technical assistance in the event of equipment disruption?

What will the weekly/monthly telework schedule be? How will the manager and coworkers be kept updated about the schedule? What happens if the schedule needs to be changed by the manager or by the employee?

What will the daily telework schedule be? Will the hours be the same as in the main office?

What are the physical attributes of the telework office, and do they conform to basic safety standards? (Use a safety checklist.)

How available does the teleworker need to be – is the telework intended to be seamless, so that phone, email, etc., are dealt with the same as in the office, or is the employee teleworking to be away from such distractions?

What is the expectation regarding the amount of notice (if any) given for reporting to the official work site, and how will such notice be provided?

How is a Telework Agreement terminated by management or an employee?

Base Denials on Business Reasons

Telework requests may be denied and Telework Agreements may be terminated. Telework is not an employee right, even if the employee is considered "eligible" by OPM standards and/or the individual agency standards. Remember

Denial and termination decisions must be based on business needs or performance, not personal reasons. For example, a manager may deny a Telework Agreement if, due to staffing issues, an employee who otherwise has portable duties must provide onsite office coverage. In this case, and whenever applicable, the denial or termination should include information about when the employee might reapply, and also if applicable, what actions the employee should take to improve his or her chance of approval. Denials should be provided in a timely manner. Managers should also review the agency's negotiated agreement(s) and telework policy to ensure they meet any applicable requirements.

Managers should provide affected employees (and keep copies of) signed written denials or terminations of Telework Agreements. These should include information about why the arrangement was denied or terminated. OPM tracks the numbers of agreements denied and/or terminated, as well as the reasons for such an action; therefore, copies should be given to the agency telework coordinator, as well.

Bargaining unit employees may file a grievance about the denial or cancellation of a telework agreement through the negotiated grievance procedure.

Use Good Performance Management Practices

Managers often ask, "How do I know my employees are working when I can't see them?" Performance standards for offsite employees are the same as performance standards for onsite employees. Management expectations of a teleworker's performance should be clearly addressed in the telework agreement. As with onsite employees, teleworkers must, and can, be held accountable for the results they produce. Good performance management techniques practiced by a manager will mean a smooth, easy transition to a telework environment. Resources for performance management are available from OPM at www.opm.gov/perform.

Make Good Decisions about Equipment

In Federal Management Regulation (FMR) Bulletin 2006-B3, Guidelines for Alternative Workplace Arrangements, GSA provides guidelines for the equipment and support that an agency may provide teleworkers. Generally, decisions are made by the agency or by individual managers regarding the ways in which teleworkers should be equipped. Managers should familiarize themselves with these guidelines and also with their agency's policy on equipment. Within those constraints, the challenge for managers is finding the right balance of budget, security, and effectiveness. Factors to consider include technology needs based on the work of the employee, agency security requirements, and budget constraints.

Remain Equitable in Assigning Work and Rewarding Performance

Managers should avoid distributing work based on "availability" as measured by physical presence, and avoid the pitfall of assuming that someone who is present and looks busy is actually accomplishing more work than someone who is not onsite. Good performance management practices are essential for telework to work effectively and equitably.

Address Security Responsibilities

Although individual employees are responsible for complying with information security requirements, managers should work with teleworkers to ensure they fully understand the relevant policies and procedures.

- ☐ Thoroughly review all telework agreements to ensure they are in compliance with agency information security policies.
- ☐ Ensure employees receive agency information systems security training.
- ☐ Work with employees to ensure they fully understand and have the technical expertise to comply with agency requirements.
- ☐ Invest in technology and equipment that can support success.
- ☐ Work with employees to develop secure systems for potentially sensitive documents and other materials.
- ☐ Track removal and return of potentially sensitive materials, such as personnel records.
- ☐ Enforce personal privacy requirements for records.

Plan for Emergencies

Telework can be an important component of agency COOP and pandemic influenza planning.

Remember

Implement telework to the greatest extent possible in the work group so systems are in place to support successful remote work in an emergency.

- ☐ Understand the agency emergency plans and management roles in executing those plans.
- ☐ Communicate expectations to all employees regarding their roles and responsibilities in relation to remote work in the event of an emergency.
- ☐ Communicate expectations both to COOP and non-COOP employees regarding what steps they need to take in case of an emergency.
- ☐ Establish communication processes to notify all employees in the event of an emergency.
- ☐ Integrate COOP and pandemic influenza expectations into Telework Agreements as appropriate.
- ☐ With the employee, assess requirements for working at home for an extended period.

☐ Determine how all employees who may telework will communicate with one another and with management to accomplish work.

Practice, Practice, Practice

! Must Do The success of an organization's telework program depends on regular, routine use. Experience is the only way to enable managers, employees, IT support, and other stakeholders to work through any technology, equipment, communications, workflow, and associated issues that may inhibit the transparency of remote work. Individuals expected to telework in an emergency situation should, with some frequency, telework under non-emergency circumstances, as well.

The Bottom Line

Managers MUST—

☐ Implement routine telework in their organization to the fullest extent possibleA**

☐ Treat employees equitably and fairly in implementing telework in their organization

☐ Identify eligible and ineligible employees using established agency criteria

☐ Include telework in COOP and other emergency response planning

No No **Managers MAY NOT**

Under normal circumstances, require that an employee work from home

Terminate a telework agreement for reasons other than business or performance

Managers MAY—

Require an employee to work at an alternative work site (e.g., a telework center) within the employee's commuting area

Terminate a telework agreement for business reasons, e.g., an employee's poor performance or a change in the nature of the work

Differences in Working at Home and at the Office

When first embarking upon hiring telecommuters, it's sometimes best to know what to avoid. In general, poor telecommuting candidates include those who:

☐ Need to meet face-to-face with people in the work place every day

☐ Operate machinery, such as in manufacturing operations

☐ Require extensive training or supervision

☐ Need a large amount of reassurance and positive reinforcement

Source: www. auxillium.com

In his book, Managing Telework, Jack Nilles also points out that, along with bureaucrats and other individuals who have inflexible work habits, socializers who need face-to-face interaction should stick to the office. He also believes that singles might do well to be cubicled if they "use [it] as a mate-meeting opportunity." However his book was published a few years before the whiz-kid world of IM, texting and blogging, not to mention Internet dating!

Screening Prospective Employees

Before determining which of your employees are eligible to telework, take the following into consideration:

☐ Hours of work

☐ Inclement weather

☐ Emergency closing

☐ Performance planning and evaluation

☐ Family and medical leave

☐ Sick leave

☐ Worker's compensation

☐ Annual leave

☐ Fair Labor Standard Act

☐ Americans with Disabilities Act (ADA)

☐ Continuity of operations

If an employee can close their door for eight hours and do their job effectively without face-to-face contact, then that job should be considered for telework. Additionally, if an employee can save enough tasks for an eight-hour interval that don't require in-person contact, then they too could be considered for telework.

Ask yourself the following questions to determine any position and employee's candidacy:

☐ Can all or part of the work be sent home with ease, speed, and confidentiality?

☐ How much face time is required with others to perform job duties?

☐ How much is the job subject to impromptu face-to-face meetings?

☐ Can the materials only be accessed at work?

☐ Can work still be performed with classified documents that must be kept in the office?

☐ What remote access capability does the teleworker have?

The Interview Process

When interviewing for telecommuting positions human resources people should not only modify what they're looking for but also who. Joye Moore, the general manager of ARO, a Kansas City, Missouri, based company that provides various industries with leading-edge business process outsourcing (BPO), had to make major adjustments when selecting customer services reps who worked at home. "When hiring an individual for the office, I focused on three things: Image, attitude and skills," she recalled. Physical appearance – in the sense that the person was neat and presentable in their dress and manners – was vital, if only to present the impression of professionalism to coworkers and clients.

Habits and mannerisms are also important when considering office work. Does the person talk loudly on the phone and with coworkers or chew with his mouth open, leaving crumbs all over the desk? Does she tend to overshare the personal details of her life or, at the opposite end, appear to be unsociable? Although such things may seem petty and irrelevant to the tasks at hand, when you're working with a team 40 hours a week in what is usually an open environment, even the smallest quirks can grate on others' nerves and eventually interfere with productivity.

They say there's no substitute for face-to-face contact, and while that's true, it can cut both ways. "You miss out on body language, which can speak volumes," continued Moore. "If the person has his arms folded or avoids your gaze, it's a good bet they're lying, and there's no way to tell that over the phone." On the other hand, however, "we've hired some really good people that we might not have otherwise considered, based on their phone skills. And for this job that's exactly what we're looking for – someone who is well-spoken, articulate, and focused. So, in a sense, we're truly hiring without discrimination." Whether the individual fails to brush their hair, prefers the window open in the dead of winter, or even works in the nude is irrelevant, as long as they get the work done. (Although with the latter, they should definitely keep it to themselves. Even though they are saving on their wardrobe, management will get very nervous if they find out!).

Hiring employees through detailed and numerous telephone interviews works well in customer service and remote sales. The "image" in this job is a clear and good-sounding voice coupled with a pleasant speaking manner. However, if the employee is meeting customers directly and/or visiting their offices, dealing extensively with individual clients remotely, (such as knowledge workers/consultants) or working in any major decision-making or influential

capacity, a face-to-face interview is best, even if it means incurring additional travel and other expenses. Another possibility is visiting the prospective worker's home office; although this also might be costly and time-consuming, you get a clear picture of their situation, resulting in fewer hiring mistakes.

A good compromise is the video interview. Enhanced and improved Web offerings and services, such as Skype, make this option increasingly feasible and cost effective. In a sense, videoconferencing offers the best of both worlds. Not does it provide face-to-face contact, giving you an idea of the interviewee's mannerisms, personality, and dress; but you can also view their home office setup.

Tips

Certain qualities are needed when making the final selection. They include:

☐ **Organization:** Because you can't physically see the individual to supervise him, "communication and organization become incredibly important," observes Merrily Orsini CEO of My Virtual Corp. "In working with a virtual team, you have meetings. You can't be late for the meeting, for instance, because it's on the telephone. In physical meetings, people oftentimes come in late and leave early. That … doesn't work virtually." Simply put, you need a person who gets the job done on time, no matter what other responsibilities she may have.

☐ **Multiple communication skills:** You need to get an idea of how well a candidate handles situations on the phone, via email, and in writing, along with "and in person." Virtual employees must be able to communicate effectively under a wide variety of circumstances – indicating for example, understanding, disagreement, the need for clarification and so forth. During the interview, "pay careful attention to tone and how well candidates get their ideas across," in all modes of communication, suggests Jeanne Allert in Training & Development magazine.

☐ **Follow-through and following directions:** "If you say you're going to do something, you really do have to do it," adds Orsini. "We ask a question in our application process about whether they like to lead or follow. The leaders tend to be the best virtual workers. I think it's because they are used to setting individual goals and tasks and meeting those." Workers who need hand-holding and constant contact are perhaps better left in the office.
On the other hand, they must also be able to follow directions and should be unafraid to ask questions. "It means clearly writing down what you need to have happen and … touching base with people along the way," she continues. "It is making very sure you understand what the task is, that the deliverable … is what the person had in mind

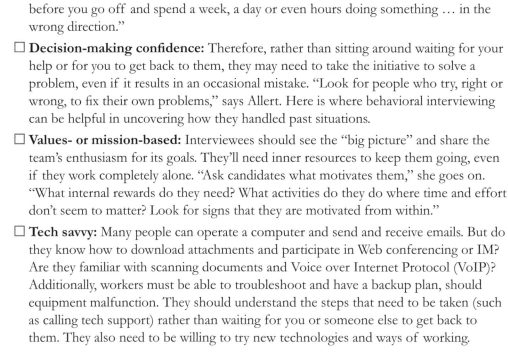

before you go off and spend a week, a day or even hours doing something … in the wrong direction."

☐ **Decision-making confidence:** Therefore, rather than sitting around waiting for your help or for you to get back to them, they may need to take the initiative to solve a problem, even if it results in an occasional mistake. "Look for people who try, right or wrong, to fix their own problems," says Allert. Here is where behavioral interviewing can be helpful in uncovering how they handled past situations.

☐ **Values- or mission-based:** Interviewees should see the "big picture" and share the team's enthusiasm for its goals. They'll need inner resources to keep them going, even if they work completely alone. "Ask candidates what motivates them," she goes on. "What internal rewards do they need? What activities do they do where time and effort don't seem to matter? Look for signs that they are motivated from within."

☐ **Tech savvy:** Many people can operate a computer and send and receive emails. But do they know how to download attachments and participate in Web conferencing or IM? Are they familiar with scanning documents and Voice over Internet Protocol (VoIP)? Additionally, workers must be able to troubleshoot and have a backup plan, should equipment malfunction. They should understand the steps that need to be taken (such as calling tech support) rather than waiting for you or someone else to get back to them. They also need to be willing to try new technologies and ways of working.

Contracts

Once you have agreed that some of your staff's duties are suitable for telework, you should focus on a Telework Agreement. In the federal government, there are many types of Telework Agreements. If your organization policies give you an option regarding agreements, consider a formal written agreement that is standardized for your organization. Such agreements take less time, benefit from trial-and-error refinement over time, avoid equity issues in your organization, and help establish a clear mutual understanding of both the arrangement and the expectations.

Usually such standardized agreements leave a few options for the specific circumstances of a given teleworker's arrangement. Regardless of whether you are simply filling in a few details in a standardized agreement or whether you are developing one from scratch, you should work together on the agreement.

Tips

As the manager, you should become familiar with the contents of typical Telework Agreements. A Telework Agreement may describe work schedules, work plans, communication avenues, performance objectives,

and other details of the telework arrangement. Your teleworker should be an informed and responsible participant in the agreement-development process.

Such steps may include:

Make sure the teleworkers understand the agency policies and procedures. Have them read the agency's telework policy to make sure they understand the telework terms and conditions. Teleworkers need to know what the guidelines and expectations are.

Ensure that the proposed arrangements meet organization and job needs and requirements.
Even though the duties lend themselves to telework, a particular position may require the worker to be in the office. Work with your staff to determine whether a telework arrangement will meet both agency and team needs. Determine if you will be able to meet performance objectives with staff teleworking.

Reiterate the performance goals already in place for the job.
Reiterate the performance goals already in place for the job to help your workers understand what is expected of them. Refer to these performance goals regularly to keep them on task.

Legal Rights of Teleworkers

As a manager, you need to be aware of all the various laws affecting workers. While most teleworkers fall under the category of "regular workers," others may have special needs, i.e., they may be older, disabled, or having issues dealing with elderly relatives/child care, among other things. The Occupational Safety and Health Administration (OSHA) and worker's compensation organizations have also gotten into the act, with mixed results.

Labor Laws for Regular (W2) Workers

Although many laws have been around for decades, with implications still being felt today, some are more recent. These laws affect all regular (W2) workers, regardless of whether they are full-time telecommuters or office personnel. The key words here are "full time."

The federal laws prohibiting job discrimination are:

Title VII of the Civil Rights Act of 1964, which prohibits employment discrimination based on race, color, religion, sex, or national origin.

The Equal Pay Act of 1963 (EPA), which protects men and women who perform substantially equal work in the same establishment from sex-based wage discrimination.

The Age Discrimination in Employment Act of 1967 (ADEA), which protects individuals age 40 or older.

Title I and Title V of the Americans with Disabilities Act of 1990 (ADA), which prohibit employment discrimination against qualified individuals with disabilities in the private sector, and in state and local governments.

Sections 501 and 505 of the Rehabilitation Act of 1973, which prohibit discrimination against qualified individuals with disabilities who work in the federal government.

The Civil Rights Act of 1991, which, among other things, provides monetary damages in cases of intentional employment discrimination.

The U.S. Equal Employment Opportunity Commission (EEOC) enforces all of these laws. EEOC also provides oversight and coordination of all federal equal employment opportunity regulations, practices, and policies. (Source: http://www.eeoc.gov/abouteeo/overview_laws.html)

Another federal law, the Family and Medical Leave Act of 1993 (FMLA) allows for up to 12 workweeks of unpaid leave during any 12-month period for eligible employees to care for a newborn child, seriously ill family members, of if they themselves develop a serious health condition, among other contingencies. (Source: http://www.dol.gov/esa/whd/fmla)

Each state has also its own laws against discrimination in addition to enforcement agencies. And although there are few laws preventing discrimination regarding sexual orientation (gays, transgender), managers should be sensitive to this area, as well. Given the recent controversy about same-sex marriage, it only follows that the rights of gays will be eventually addressed in the workplace. The cold reality is that many of these issues, particularly relating to age and sex, do come into play in decisions regarding hiring and promotion more often then they should.

To protect themselves legally, managers should avoid knowing the employee's age, sexual orientation or even family situation. Although this may seem somewhat stringent, consider the fact that upon legal review, you as manager may be perceived as having utilized this information to make decisions on which employee to promote, terminate, and so forth. Information about equal labor laws can be found at www.eeoc.gov; most states also have a specific Website for their laws. Source: Management Basics, Sandra Gurvis

Additionally, the Fair Labor Standards Act (FLSA) establishes minimum wage, overtime pay, recordkeeping, and child labor standards affecting full-time and part-time workers in the

private sector and in federal, state, and local governments. Covered nonexempt workers are entitled to a minimum wage of not less than $7.25 per hour effective July 24, 2009. Overtime pay at a rate of not less than one and one-half times their regular rates of pay is required after 40 hours of work in a workweek. The FLSA applies to telecommuters as well; for example, you must pay time-and-a-half to nonexempt employees who work overtime, whether they are home or office-based.

Teleworking and Unions

Two teleworking issues that most concern unions are equity and productivity. First, unions consider teleworking as an employee benefit. But since not all employees are always selected to telework, some unions view telework as inequitable.

Second, unions worry that telework will become a high-tech version of sweatshops where productivity is minutely measured, and production goals are set at ever-increasing levels. The organizations with labor agreements and telework programs credit their success to working with their unions to resolve these issues from the beginning.

Integrating Teleworkers and Office Workers

Telecommuters may experience resistance and resentment from office co-workers and in some cases even clients who know about their work-from-home status. They can expect everything from clients who call after hours to discuss matters that can be handled 9 a.m. to 5 p.m. to downright envy from peers who feel trapped in office jobs. However, managers can and must take steps to avoid "tele-resentment."

Make sure that the work is properly and evenly distributed and that office employees are aware of exactly what the teleworker is doing, and when. Communication is key, otherwise the teleworker becomes "invisible" and cut out of the loop. Managers should constantly emphasize and reinforce the fact that everyone is a member of the team, despite the diversity in the working conditions and physical locations.

Must Do

And sometimes office workers do have a legitimate beef. "In my workshops for soon-to-be teleworkers, I urge them to be sensitive to what could result in their colleagues having to put out all the fires in the office," states David Fleming, organizer the California Task Force on Interactive Telecommunications in Government. To help forestall resentment, managers can assign teleworkers their fair share of the more routine duties.

Another way of boosting team morale and facilitating communications is through a forum or blog where everyone can discuss telecommuting, office scheduling and workload problems. As mentioned earlier, software is available so all members of the team can have access.

Arranging for a specific day or time period for "virtual brainstorming" by all team members helps managers identify any ongoing issues before they become a full-blown crisis.

Set specific boundaries. Along with clearly identifying workloads and setting goals, managers should make sure that teleworkers know what hours they are to be available, and that they are responsible for being reachable during this time. Coworkers and clients should also be aware of when the teleworkers are "off duty." The cell phone has eliminated many of these boundaries, so it's good to set them in the initial work plan.

Tips

Arrange face-to-face meetings, especially at the beginning. Most teleworkers are glad of an occasional excuse to get out of the office, especially if it provides a chance to socialize and become acquainted with the other employees and visit the organization. Putting a "face" on things not only increases comfort levels (in most cases, anyway) but provides all parties with a sense of being vested in the project or organization.

Step Three: Organization – Getting Together a Game Plan

Logistics of Meetings, Virtual and Physical

Thanks to technology, we can now have virtual meetings with many people in different locations and time zones around the world. The problem is in finding a time that is acceptable to everyone. When proposing a meeting you have to be flexible over timing, unless it is urgent that it is held as soon as possible.

Having agreed on a meeting time, you then need a clear agenda which can be distributed to people in advance. Time is money, so stick to the agenda and discuss only the points relevant to it – don't get sidetracked.

To paraphrase the late, great humorist James Thurber, "Are meetings necessary?" The answer, whether your team is completely virtual or partially office-based, is probably "yes." However the good news is that you have a number of alternatives to choose from, ranging from old-school conference calls and face-to-face meetings to cutting-edge virtual conferencing and more.

Many variables come into play – the urgency of the message, the complexity of the information, and what you're trying to achieve. The latter also relates to who are you talking to – you might use a different mode of communication for a potential client or a distant collaborator than for members of a close-knit team.

Telephone

In spite of technology, the telephone remains the basic form of communication. Just look at the iPhone – underneath its touch screen and video capabilities, including software that can give the impression that you're drinking champagne from it, it serves the same purpose as the device invented by Alexander Graham Bell in 1876. So there, Steve Jobs!

With the advent of the cell phone you can reach out and touch anyone, anywhere, at any time. This can be both a good and bad thing, but is mostly beneficial to telecommuters who need to be reached "from a distance" whether they are based in a foreign country or en route

to a child's ballet lesson. Such contact, however, should be limited to the mutually-agreed upon boundaries set by the job. There's no excuse for calling someone when they're "off duty" unless it's an emergency.

The most common form of telephone meeting is a teleconference. This allows several users to dial into a single number and is either hosted internally or through a third-party service provider. Along with connecting everyone simultaneously, it offers "real-time" interaction and is generally fairly inexpensive.

However, there are disadvantages. You are "not always clear who's talking," states author Kelly Pate Dwyer of Bnet.com. Also, "time lags result in people talking at the same time. Callers often multitask, so their attention is divided. If most of the group is in one location, people calling in feel left out of the conversation." Additionally, it's "hard to show people what you're talking about or give visual presentations."

Therefore, teleconferences work best with smaller groups or teams who know each other, for shorter meetings and/or planning sessions. Dwyer recommends sending out an agenda or a visual aid beforehand and being very specific during the meeting as to the item referenced and/or its actual location.

All team members need to have the proper equipment so they can clearly hear what's being said. They should also be trained as to the technical side of teleconferencing so they can to join in and add others, if necessary.

Etiquette is another important area. Assign meeting roles and make sure participants identify themselves when talking. Allowing everyone a chance to speak, even if it means taking an informal "roll call" when decisions are being made, is also vital; silence does not necessarily indicate agreement. Team members need to weigh in with their opinion. Also, when someone is inadvertently interrupted or two people start talking at the same time, the person who interrupts should apologize and allow the other party to complete their thoughts before giving them theirs.

Background noise can create major embarrassments, particularly if the conference is taking place over speakerphone or microphone. Depending upon the sensitivity of the equipment, even the most ambient sounds of shuffling papers, personal noises (such as sneezing), or a neighbor's loud music can be heard by all. Participants should be made aware of this potential beforehand so they can put the speakerphone on "mute" when they're not talking.

Also keep conversation to the subject at hand. "Topic drift" can happen more frequently when people know each other and start chatting about mutual interests and unrelated subjects. This can add unnecessary time to the meeting and be counterproductive to completing the agenda.

Meeting Roles for Teleconferences

Leader: Organizes and facilitates the meeting, making sure the agenda is covered in the allotted amount of time. This can be the manager or (preferably) a team member who has a vested interest in the topic.

Gatekeeper: Makes sure that everyone participates as equally as possible. Along with encouraging reticent members to speak up, this may mean squelching those who talk too much. ("Thanks for the information, John. Lisa, what do you think about this?")

Scribe: Takes notes during the meeting and distributes them afterwards; is responsible for making sure that all important information is included, such as key decisions and action items.

Participant: Although this may seem obvious, participants should understand their importance in the meeting. They need to honestly express opinions, stay on track with the agenda, and follow teleconferencing etiquette.

These roles can be rotated, so everyone gets a chance to experience the different responsibilities. Acting in the different capacities provides team members with a sense of ownership, as well as building communications and leadership skills.

Adapted from The Distance Manager, by Kimball Fisher and Maurine Duncan Fisher. New York: McGraw-Hill pp. 157.

Videoconferencing

Remember "The Jetsons?" Perhaps not, but back in the 1960s when that TV show was in its heyday, George Jetson and his family communicated by videophones and other virtual technology. While videophones haven't quite yet reached the average American household, its first cousin, videoconferencing, pretty much has. Although the equipment and technology has a way to go and can be clumsy and awkward, it has become somewhat cost-effective. All you need are a video camera or Webcam; computer monitor, television or projector; microphones; loudspeakers hooked up to the monitor or telephone and a data transfer system and voila – you can communicate live! The data transfer system can be either an analog or digital telephone network, LAN or Internet.

Another, more expensive videoconferencing option is a dedicated system, where all the components are combined in a single piece of equipment. Consisting of a remote control

video camera which can zoom in and pan wherever needed, it provides better overall quality of communications. Systems can be large, small, or even portable. Cameras can also be posted in conference rooms or workstations, and voice activation allows the camera to focus on whoever is speaking.

Videoconferences are particularly helpful in that you can see the person's expressions, gestures and general body language – as long as the images remain sharp and clear and there are no delays in transmission. It can be especially useful when hiring and interviewing, and is a good alternative in introducing team members who are geographically disbursed. It can also take the place of some time-consuming and expensive travel.

However, if you're willing to spend big bucks you can purchase telepresence, a high-definition, high-bandwidth version of videoconferencing. This utilizes multiple oversized plasma screens and speakers and real-time audio, not only allowing for clarity of expression and eye contact, but eliminating audio delay. However, it requires dedicated conference rooms, high-bandwidth audio, and a modern Voice over IP (VOIP) switching infrastructure and, because many systems operate on proprietary networks, it usually only works for meetings within the company.

And even telepresence doesn't overcome the fact many people are uncomfortable in front of a "live" camera and may not perform at their best. If the person sees himself onscreen presenting, it can even be more distracting and inhibiting.

Still videoconferencing can be useful, if all team members are trained in equipment and presentation; time limits are observed (no more than two hours); and the "mute" features are utilized when participants aren't talking, as microphones pick up all sound. Kimball Fisher and Maureen Duncan Fisher, authors of The Distance Manager (New York: McGraw-Hill, 2001) advise encouraging participants to be creative in their use of the media, allowing team members, for example, to zoom in on the individual who is speaking and utilize "show and tell" video clips. "When people have more control over the technology, they are more likely to use it effectively."

Internet Conferencing

The Internet is expanding and evolving as are the ways of utilizing it for conferences and meetings. However, the same rules of etiquette and methods of organizing meetings discussed earlier apply here, as well.

There are several different kinds of Internet conferences. For a Web conference, users login to a "real time" Website or software program, such as LiveMeeting (an earlier version of

NetMeeting) or Windows Meeting Space. Various media can be used, from slides to live video to text chat to audio VOIP to whiteboard annotation. The electronic equivalent of a chalk and blackboard, whiteboard systems enable participants to simultaneously view one or more users drawing on an onscreen blackboard or running an application that provides a visual of same. Whiteboards are especially helpful in documenting the results or action decisions of the meeting. They are usually jotted down by the scribe, enabling all to see and agree/disagree with various points while the meeting is taking place.

Although Web conferencing allows team members to troubleshoot, share documents, and collaborate remotely across time, space, and even cultures, technical difficulties frequently pop up, often due to the incompatibilities of the various technologies or the fact that one vital feature isn't working, such as a microphone. A team member may have unintentionally downloaded a program that disabled certain Web meeting functions (anyone who has ever spent time on a computer has experienced this marriage-made-in-hell incompatibility between programs). A quick run-through before the actual meeting gets underway can alleviate many of these issues.

Additionally, complicated discussions can get bogged down, so it's important to keep visuals interesting and utilize the polling and messaging functions. With polling – an electronic form of taking attendance -- the "main" computer interrogates its connected terminals in a round-robin sequence. Users then send a response. Regardless of what method you use, make sure participants stay engaged by typing email comments or using the audio portion to indicate their opinions and involvement.

As with all meetings, set an agenda and time limit, along with providing sufficient advance notice. This is especially important with a far-flung team that is engaged in complex tasks. Team members need time to prepare, especially for the complicated and in-depth discussions that often take place during these types of meetings. And although this may seem a small thing, make sure to have the right time and a specific date: For example, March 23, 2010, at 1:30 p.m., Eastern Standard Time. Just saying "Monday" might cause confusion for someone in Australia or Asia who is 24 hours ahead or behind.

In contrast to synchronous Web conferencing is the Wiki or ftp site, which allows for the exchange of knowledge and information by participants at different times. Basically an online archive of large, linked files for team and client access, the Wiki allows participants to add, modify, and update information. Wikipedia, the definitive but often controversial encyclopedia of information on the Internet, is an example of this.

File transfer protocols (ftps) are more stagnant but allow users to download information at their leisure. Both can be helpful in gathering feedback from all users and for project planning, although maintenance and implementation can be time-consuming and difficult. It's also best to designate a gatekeeper who will make sure that updates don't override each other in the Wiki, and information stays current in both.

Internet conferencing also utilizes collaboration technology, a project-specific online workspace that allows colleagues to exchange and modify information. It is especially useful for brainstorming, customer presentations, and storing company and client information in a central location, and works well with small, tech-savvy groups.

Programs, such as Microsoft SharePoint, provide a single workspace for teams to coordinate schedules, organize documents, and participate in discussions – within the organization and over the Extranet. This can be done asynchronously, a boon to team members in different time zones.

When to Meet "Face to Face"

Face-to-Face Meetings

If at possible, these should occur during these circumstances:

Initial interview: While not always necessary – depending upon the situation, phone interviews may be equally if not more effective as discussed in earlier chapters – the initial interview should be in person, especially if the potential employee is in a customer-facing role.

Project kickoff: Getting off to a good start is important to a team's success and sets the tone for the entire project. Along with building a common understanding and purpose and helping the team coalesce into a solid unit, this meeting can "define the team's charter, set goals, establish operating guidelines, describe communication preferences, and review boundaries," according to authors Kimball Fisher and Maureen Duncan Fisher.

Mileposts: Especially with a long-term project, it can be difficult to stay focused. But periodically bringing the team together provides an added boost and impetus to "git'r done." Plus, teams can stay current on problems and maintain a sense of connection and trust. If possible, teams should meet regularly; ideally, once a quarter.

Wrap-ups or celebrations: Along with celebrating a project's completion, these can "prepare the team to be more effective in future assignments," the authors say. By meeting face-to-face, workers can build upon each other's ideas and review and analyze problems,

decisions, and other issues. Such in-person meetings also provide much-needed recognition and networking opportunities.

Conflict resolution, performance reviews, and discussions: Anything relating to performance is best discussed in person to establish rapport and eliminate confusion and misinterpretations. A conflict among team members is likely best resolved face-to-face, if possible.

Doing Business in Different Countries and Time Zones

Remember that you may be having your morning coffee sitting in your office, but the person on the other end of the teleconference might have had to set his alarm clock and get up in the middle of the night to take part. Be considerate when arranging meeting times, and vary the times so that the same people are not inconvenienced every time.

Remember

If you make a lot of calls or have meetings with team members and customers overseas, install automatic software on your computer so that you always know what time it is in their time zone.

As communications increase and the world shrinks (at least virtually), the argument for doing business overseas becomes increasingly stronger, even for smaller companies. But as anyone who has tried to work with or in a foreign culture knows, such dealings can be fraught with complications.

In addition to the differences in language, ways of doing business, customs and time zones, variances in infrastructure can present challenges. These can range from wide disparities in telecommunications systems which fail to support technology (for example, hampering interactive software) to inconsistencies in availability and dependability of mobile and/or land lines. Another issue is the quality of support and services – import restrictions can slow down the repair of vital equipment, as can inadequately trained or a scarcity of technicians. The cost of importing replacement parts might be exorbitant, as well.

Also, consider how the population is distributed. Are teleworkers concentrated in small apartments (with limited or no space for home offices) and/or villages where cable and Internet access are much less common than in bigger cities? If so, then you may be faced with the cost and requirements of establishing a telework center.

In addition to time zones, what are the discrepancies in work customs? For example, countries in the Mediterranean area of Europe tend to take two-hour lunch breaks, while

Germans rarely if ever work on the weekends. And it's well-known that most of the rest of the world takes much longer than the U.S. in getting projects done and making decisions.

You'll also need to address issues relating to taxes and statutory compliance. For example: Who pays taxes on the salaries of overseas workers, and to which country? And, what happens about currency? If workers are located in India, will they be paid in rupees or U.S. dollars? Another sticking point is whether or not workers are to be considered regular employees or independent contractors. Each country has different laws and requirements, raising even more questions regarding healthcare and other benefits.

However, gaps between countries are narrowing, especially regarding technology. Ironically, Asia and Europe are ahead of North America in terms of sophistication and speed of Internet access, while Sweden and Finland lead the world in cellular services. So-called Third World countries in Africa and the Middle East have increasingly widespread mobile phone technology (although land lines might not be as readily available); in recent years, both show several hundred percent's worth of growth in use of Internet technology. Trade agreements have also helped lower the price of some equipment.

None of these obstacles is insurmountable, especially if you're flexible and willing to use your imagination. For example, one independent contractor, while in remote areas of Scotland, took along his laptop, cell phone and trusty international calling card. When attempts to connect with clients via the first two failed, he was able to locate that almost extinct species of communication in the U.S., a phone booth, and do business from there.

Case Study: Making Diversity Work

Since 1994, IBM in Phoenix, Arizona, has utilized a telecommuting program involving approximately one-fourth of its full-time employees. Jobs ranged from sales to marketing to technicians and systems consultants to customer service. Along with developing hardware and software specifically for telecommuters, they allowed for flexible work settings (desks at customer sites, offsite telework center, and work from home options) and created handbooks/policies geared for telecommuters. They also provided some equipment.

According to manager Skip Richards, "Our telework program allows IBM to be at the forefront of the technology industry. It has enabled us to have a regional, instead of a geographic organizational structure. Now, people are managed in different cities across geographic boundaries."

Additionally, "our telecommuters are more culturally diverse. There are fewer cliques. It has created much wider diversity in IBM's company culture." Telecommuting is also no longer considered an oddity. "Since there are so many teleworkers at IBM, it doesn't affect them too much. If employees want to telework, the resources are available."

Setting Goals and Keeping on Track

Goal setting means identifying and defining the specific results required. Goals are important. Unless you know where you are going, you may end up someplace you'd rather not be or someplace other than where you want to go. Have you ever been given a vague "goal" and been told later that you didn't do what was required? Such an experience was undoubtedly frustrating for everyone involved.

The ability to establish and define effective results-oriented goals is central to good management and should underlie everything you, as a manager, do. The most successful managers know where they are going, even though they may at times be unsure about the best way to get there. They decide what the future should look like and work with their team to make that vision a reality.

Remember

Planning

The goal sets out where we are going, while the plan defines how we are going to get there. One approach is to say, "We have our goal, so let's just get on with it." But that can easily result in duplication of effort or in an important task being missed because everybody thought someone else was doing it. You need to plan. A plan subdivides the work and ensures that resources are used effectively.

Focus on specific activities rather than the "big picture." This is the most important aspect of goal-setting – breaking it into small, manageable pieces. For example, if sales in your department are down 25 percent and you look at it all at once, you might think, "That's terrible! How can we pull ourselves out of this tailspin?"

However, when you examine each aspect of the problem, patterns begin to emerge. In researching the product, you might find that the sales force isn't up to date on the latest information. From that, you could set a goal to make sure they're trained in the newest technology.

Or you may find that the sales team is slacking on the number of calls they're making. Set a goal for them of X number of calls per week. Finally, you might see that you've lost several key customers. Your new goal would be to revisit those customers and try to find out what went wrong, understand their needs, and see if they have been met or just not understood. Now you've got a clear idea of what caused the drop in sales. Additional goals to help increase sales might include:

1. The department will send out emails and written material to new and current customers describing the department's "enhanced" and "updated" services.

2. Each sales rep will research and find five to seven potential new customers over the next month.

3. You will offer a discount to former customers to tempt them back into using your products and services.

A word of caution: It's best to keep lists of goals short, containing no more than five items. Setting too many goals will only dilute their effectiveness and create confusion. Find the three or four most important goals, and work on them first. Once you've achieved these goals, you can add to the list.

Concentrate on Results Rather Than Activities

Lists of goals often focus on a series of activities rather than on the results to be achieved. For instance, "Investigate the production shortfall," "Ensure that staff are adequately trained and developed," "Prepare a recommendation on departmental staffing." These are activities rather than goals.

Then there's the problem of corporate-speak. "Optimize productivity ratios for the benefit of the organization," "Maximize staff morale." Sounds impressive, but what the heck does it mean? People often use words, such as "optimize" and "maximize," because they have no idea what can realistically be achieved and may not have thought through what needs to be done.

Goals are much clearer when they are positively stated as results. In the example from the previous paragraph you might ask, "Why am I saying we need to investigate productivity (or whatever)?" This question indicates that you must change the focus from an activity into a result. For example, "We need to investigate productivity to find out why there is a 10-percent shortfall on product X and correct that shortfall within a week." Then ask yourself, "Have I now clearly identified the actual result I need?"

Essential Factors of Goals (MARC)

Goals should be:

Measurable: A goal should be measurable to ensure that the person knows when he has achieved it. Some things are easier to measure than others. The measurement can be subjective – "Provide an adequate personnel service to internal customers." You can measure the goal by asking those customers periodically about the service.

Achievable: The goal should be seen as achievable by the person designated to carry it out. One person's challenge can be another's impossibility if their respective levels of skill

or knowledge are markedly different. In the modern workplace, results are often achieved through collaboration with personnel not under your direct control. You should not shy away from establishing goals in these cases, but rather call upon your skills of managing without authority.

Result-oriented: Ensure that objectives are stated as results, not activities. Give a deadline by which the results must be achieved.

Clear: The goal must be understood (and agreed on) by the person responsible for achieving it.

Prioritize for Maximum Effect

Have you ever found yourself in a situation where you have several things to do, but you know that in the time available you cannot attend to all of them satisfactorily?

That's called "a clash of priorities." Often to the harassed manager it seems like all the pressing matters are priorities. If you ask your own manager which of these tasks is more important you may get a non-answer: "They all are." So it's up to you to decide or make a best guess.

You can avoid this problem. When discussing a list of goals, include a column headed "Priority," and rate each goal as "high," "medium," or "low." Bear in mind that "low" does not mean "unimportant;" it just means less important than the "mediums" or "highs."

In the event of a clash of priorities, the "highs" automatically take precedence. Most of the time, your employees won't need to refer questions of priority back to you. Upfront identification of tasks as medium and low priorities makes it easy to reprioritize what can "move off your plate" as other, more pressing tasks materialize.

One final point to note is that priorities of ongoing objectives can alter over time, so review priority ratings regularly.

Tips

Encourage Your Team to Suggest Their Own Goals

Some managers believe that the only person who should set goals for the team is the manager herself. So goals are handed down, rather like the two tablets of stone given to Moses on Mount Sinai, with little opportunity for discussion. There are two reasons behind this thinking:

1.   "It's my responsibility as the manager."

2.   "If I ask them to do it, they will set themselves easy goals that won't achieve what I need."

As manager, you are certainly responsible for ensuring that the goal is set, but that doesn't necessarily mean you have to set it. As for the second point, it is a natural fear but is usually unfounded. Most people like a challenge and, if asked, will usually suggest complex but realistic objectives for themselves.

You need commitment to the goals, rather than simple acceptance. The best way to ensure this commitment is to involve the team members in setting their objectives.

Prior to any discussion of goals, ask them to think first about the key results areas in their job and then to suggest some objectives they can set. Let them think about these things and then discuss them further.

It will also help if you explain MARC. The discussion then becomes an exchange of views – yours and the employee's. Wherever possible, agree to the employee's proposed goal if it meets your needs and is realistic for her. If her objective does not meet your requirements, you will need to explain (and prove) why, so that she learns for next time.

The manager should also encourage and provide motivation to the staff regarding their ability to achieve "stretch goals," objectives that are seemingly unattainable using current resources. Developing an environment where risk-taking – and giving team members the knowledge, tools, and support to think creatively – is fundamental to achieving stretch goals.

Make someone responsible for each task, and set a deadline.

Consider the plans you already have, in addition to essential tasks.

Do they also show who is responsible for the various tasks?

Do they show the deadline for each task?

Many plans leave out these important elements. In worst-case scenarios, the people who have to carry out the plan aren't even given a copy of the plan! Without specific responsibilities, confusion can easily arise … "I thought you were doing that part!"

 Without specific deadlines for each main task, the whole plan can easily slip behind and then fail to achieve the original goal.

Remember

For each specific task:

Decide and agree on a single person who will be responsible for ensuring that this particular task is successfully achieved. Joint responsibilities are risky, for they can lead to confusion.

Decide and agree on the deadline by which that task must be successfully completed. As the individual selected will have responsibility for ensuring that the task is completed on time, their commitment is usually vital. So agree on the goals with them at the planning stage.

In setting goals, remember to break them down into small, manageable pieces. You will then begin to discern a pattern and can identify specific areas needing attention. You can then decide which actions will help you achieve your goal and/or solve the problem.

Organizing Workflow

If you're dealing with the additional challenge of working with telecommuters – whether they be your entire staff or only a few people – managing workflow may seem even more daunting. Before setting goals and measuring milestones, consider your feelings towards working with telecommuters. Are you frustrated with the idea of getting the job done from a distance – with little or limited control over workers' schedules – and not actually being able to walk around and see them perform their tasks? Do you feel employees are not responsible enough to work on their own? As Jack M. Nilles, "the father of telecommuting," pointed out there are two halves of telemanagement: quality communications and establishing trust. The latter can relate to trust in your own leadership skills, as well as in the employees themselves.

One way to develop confidence in leadership is to focus on outcomes rather than processes. When viewed that way, managing telecommuters is not really that much different from managing office workers. Managers who communicate clearly and offer direct feedback, along with providing well-designed and measurable objectives, are generally effective and successful, no matter how their employees get the job done. And studies have borne this out. When asked how they measured productivity for their telecommuters (as opposed to their office workers), managers at the National Center for Transportation and Industrial Productivity at the New Jersey Institute of Technology (NJIT) replied they used similar processes for both. In many organizations, in-house and remote employees are managed in the exact same manner, using identical performance and evaluation standards.

Tips

Setting Clear Performance Standards

When formulating the performance standards, focus on the final product rather than the processes used to achieve it. It is of no concern to management how teleworkers are dressed, whether they snack at their desks while working (as long as the client/customer doesn't hear

them eating), or whether they're walking around instead of sitting down. The point is, as long as they fill their quotas, which result in satisfied customers/increased sales, they're doing their jobs.

Successful teleworking programs require consistent performance standards for all employees, whether they are onsite or offsite, telecommuters or office-based. So when designing goals and objectives, make sure you are clear on:

☐ What must be done

☐ Why it must be done

☐ How well it must be done

☐ By when it must be done

☐ What constitutes a job that is complete

Ask yourself what elements of the position will provide the most effective and efficient operations. And what is the desired end result? You also need to communicate to employees how these goals tie into the business plan of the overall department. This provides a sense of ownership, as well as a feeling that they are part of the overall team.

Measures should be objective and focus on four factors: quality, quantity, timeliness, and cost efficiency. Quality concerns the amount of errors, omissions, and complaints tolerated over a specific amount of time; while quantity is the measurable unit of production. Timeliness focuses on deadlines for tasks and amount of turnaround time required. Cost efficiency deals with staying within the constraints of a budget and being accountable for monies spent.

There are several ways of setting performance standards and goals; many books have been written on the topic. The point is that you want to make sure telecommuters don't waste time and resources pursuing wrong objectives, but instead go after the specified goals. The more clearly you describe objectives, the less time you will need to spend explaining them, as has been traditionally done through informal workplace encounters or meetings. It is also a more efficient way of doing business.

However, some goals are easier to define than others. Goals are clear-cut and easily quantifiable for production-oriented jobs, such as sales, customer service, and forms/file processing, whereas it is more difficult to pinpoint goals for jobs, such as Web design and project management.

Goal Posts

Supervisors and telecommuters need to agree upon goals, which should have the following characteristics.

Clearly defined and specific: i.e., make 20 calls for every four-hour workday, or sell six policies a month, rather than "increase sales."

Measurable, as in the above example: That way the person will know what he is achieving and how far he has progressed.

Challenging, yet doable: One person's challenge can be another's impossibility. If the worker knows upfront what she is up against, then she will know whether she can accomplish it. By its very nature, a challenge allows more variation in the range of outcomes, so it may not always work for all aspects of routine jobs.

Results-oriented and clear: The worker knows the end result and understands what is expected of him.

If there is more than one goal, you may need to help workers prioritize; that is, rate the goals as high, medium, or low. Telecommuters in particular may need guidance with this, especially in the beginning.

Establishing Rules and Boundaries

Another important aspect of workload management is developing work plans and task schedules. Whenever you make an assignment, clearly define what is to be accomplished and the schedule for completing the task. As with office workers, telecommuters should acknowledge the assignment, agree to the schedule, and take responsibility for finishing it in the appropriate manner. (See, it's not so different after all!)

Work plans ensure that the worker remains "on course," as well as providing clear and measurable results. It should also be made apparent that the worker's performance evaluation is based upon the plan. It also allows for helpful "one on one" coaching time, since you are both involved in developing the plan and can make modifications, if necessary.

Work plans should include the following:

☐ The objective(s) that will be met

☐ Tasks to be accomplished

☐ The product to be developed as necessary

☐ The timeframe for completing tasks

☐ A schedule for accomplishing interim milestones (for longer-term assignments)

☐ Who else needs to be involved, and what resources may be needed

☐ Criteria or standards for evaluating performance.

Scheduling

In an ideal world – at least for the telecommuter – the worker establishes his own schedule. However, real life is quite different and you may be called upon to provide parameters as to when duties should be performed. This is for the convenience of all concerned – the company's goals; the other team members, some of who may be office workers and/or on a different time schedule or zone; and of course, your own workload needs. So it's important to sit down with the employee and develop a schedule that will work for everyone, with a minimum of inconvenience. What you don't want is to have the teleworker absent or unavailable when you need him the most. So communicate this at the beginning of the arrangement.

Consider the following guidelines when scheduling:

☐ What are the core hours that you'll need telecommuters to be available?

☐ Is there any flexibility in these hours?

☐ How often do they need to call in or check their voicemail and emails?

☐ How quickly do they need to return messages?

☐ How often will they need to communicate with you and/or other members of the team?

Depending upon the job and its requirements, the worker may need to come into the office or be available for extra hours. If this is the case, it should also be mentioned when doing scheduling.

Arrange teleworkers' schedules primarily to meet the business needs of the department, not the convenience of the teleworkers. The latter is important, but is not the main objective. Plan your teleworkers' schedules with the same logic as you arrange vacation schedules; once again, coverage is more important than convenience. Flexibility on both sides is crucial; teleworkers must understand there are times when you'll need them in the office on a planned telework day, and you as manager should be open to their requests for schedule changes.

At certain times you may need to suspend telework for everyone, and it has nothing to do with any individual's performance. For example, if you have a new employee starting you might want everyone available to meet and help mentor that person. Or you might anticipate

a short-term workload crunch and need everyone available because task assignments will be changing too quickly to allow for even planned telework days.

The optimal telework scheduling blends the needs of the department and its customers with the preferences of the teleworkers. The more adaptable everyone remains, the better the chances of making best use of telework opportunities. A "cookie-cutter" approach with all teleworkers adhering to a rigid, pre-set schedule can be counterproductive. By its very nature, telework is supposed to be flexible.

Remember

Developing Work Plans and Task Schedules

The telework agreement defines the type of work to be completed at home, but may not include every individual assignment that comes up in the course of routine operations. Whenever you make an assignment, whether to a teleworker or to an office employee, clearly define what is to be accomplished and the schedule for completing the task. Your employee should acknowledge the assignment, agree to the schedule, and take responsibility for completing it as expected.

This provides an excellent example of how managing teleworkers really isn't much different from managing office staff. Managing from a distance consists of the same basic processes, but requires some extra work to make sure the teleworker is performing his/her duties and remains part of the team. But, in return, managers of teleworkers invariably report that they also become more efficient managers of staff working in the office.

A structured work plan fits well with telework for three reasons. First, it greatly reduces the chance that the teleworker will go off course on a task. Second, it is a good way to give the manager an opportunity to coach and develop the employee by involving him/her in the process of developing the plan. Third, the time invested in developing the plan pays off later when it's time to assess performance. Having the plan in hand provides an instant benchmark for helping manager and teleworker determine how well the task has been done.

Structured work plans typically involve the following elements:

☐ The objective that will be met

☐ Tasks to be accomplished

☐ The product to be developed

☐ The timeframe for completing tasks

☐ A schedule for accomplishing interim milestones (for longer-term assignments)

☐ Who else needs to be involved, and what resources may be needed

☐ Criteria or standards for evaluating performance.

Remember Work plans don't have to impose a big burden on the manager's role, and definitely should not replace any existing work management or tracking procedures in use. The goal is not to add in more paperwork and bureaucracy, but to make best use of available resources or systems and tailor them for the purpose of guiding the teleworker's performance.

The following is an example of a standard scheduling agreement:

FLEXIPLACE WORK SCHEDULE

Employee: _____

Date: _____

Type of Flexiplace Schedule _ Fixed _ As Needed

Type of Alternative Work Schedule*
_ Flexitour _ Gliding Schedule _ Compressed Schedule: _ 5-4-9 _ 4-10

Week 1: Office	Alt Work site	Start Time	Finish Time
Mon:			
Tue:			
Wed:			
Thu:			
Fri:			

* If you select the flexitour or compressed schedule, indicate your proposed start and finish times in the space provided. It is not necessary to indicate start and finish times if you select the gliding schedule.

Adapted from the Department of Education Flexiplace Program, www.telework.gov/policies/education.asp.

In some telecommuting situations, workers are scheduled at different times of the day in "shifts" to meet the needs of clients. This is made clear during the interview process, and managers work with them to find the shift that best meets their needs. For example, if a call center employee has children in school, she can opt for a 9 a.m.-3 p.m. shift to accommodate her lifestyle.

Measuring Productivity

Measuring and managing productivity can be difficult. Productivity is a ratio between hours worked and units of output. That is fine when dealing with manual work because there are concrete outcomes, but it becomes more problematic when dealing with white-collar

workers whose output is dependent on their knowledge. At the very least, the teleworker should be as productive as someone working in the office doing the same job. In reality, the teleworker, free from other distractions, is often more productive. However, procedures need to be put in place to measure this.

Productivity can be measured by establishing specific objectives for both individuals and the group. You then judge performance according to how well individuals and groups meet these objectives. Another way to determine productivity is to solicit feedback from customers or coworkers who receive work performed by the teleworkers.

These two examples show why simplistic, quantity-oriented productivity measures are inadequate:

A customer service agent who takes incoming calls from customers can handle more calls per hour than anyone else - but in doing so, he gives short, impolite answers and doesn't take time to fully understand the nature of the callers' problems.

An auditor who visits field locations to do inspections always completes the assigned inspections on time - but she often leaves out important elements in her inspection reports and is late getting the reports filed.

In both cases, it may seem that these employees are being very productive. In fact, they are producing a lot of output but, in doing so, are failing on various quality or task-completion measures. Knowledge workers need to know what their personal "productivity dashboard" looks like, and this is especially important for teleworkers who require guidance as to what indicators to concentrate on.

In many cases teleworkers may already have their own computer and Internet connection at home, but if the computer and software are incompatible with office systems, or if there are security or virus-protection concerns, it may be false economy to allow or even require them to use their own equipment. Since budget realities may limit your ability to provide computers for all teleworkers, it may be better to have fewer teleworkers who are properly equipped, than to increase the numbers, but seriously limit their effectiveness by having them work with substandard technology.

A rule of thumb – and even that doesn't always work – is to compare the productivity of office workers with that of telecommuters. That is, they should do the same amount of work within the same time constraints. Often, with fewer distractions, the telecommuter can be even more productive. But, once again, quality may be in issue. Depending upon the nature of the work, the office employee might just be rubber-stamping or doing tasks by rote – or be

overworked and pulled in too many directions – while the telecommuter can clearly focus on the task at hand, due to his work-at-home environment, increased morale, and motivation to maintain the arrangement.

You can, however, establish procedures to help measure productivity that give specific objectives for employees to meet, individually and as a group. You can then judge the group's performance, and the performances of individual employees, according to how well they meet these objectives. The procedures can be used as general guidelines for both office workers and telecommuters.

The following are some elements of productivity measurement for knowledge workers. Rather than looking at a single measure, they should be evaluated cumulatively, with an eye to the "big picture" of the end product or results.

- ☐ Quality of work produced
- ☐ Quantity of work produced
- ☐ Timeliness of work products submitted
- ☐ Timely and appropriate communication with managers and coworkers
- ☐ Timely and appropriate responses to email, phone calls, and requests from managers and coworkers
- ☐ Written or verbal progress reports or reviews
- ☐ Ability to "juggle" multiple tasks simultaneously

Another way to determine productivity is to solicit feedback from customers or coworkers. This can be implemented through surveys; monitoring, such as recording customer service calls and/or having the supervisor listen in at periodic intervals; or follow-up phone calls, letters, or emails.

Training

Manager Training:

Telework can be advantageous for managers in many ways, including the following:

Do you need to attract or perhaps retain qualified employees? Telework may be an appealing incentive for those who value this form of flexibility.

Do you want to help employees do their best work? Telework can provide blocks of uninterrupted time so they can concentrate with fewer distractions, which typically results in more and/or better work produced.

Step Three: Organization – Getting Together a Game Plan

Are you concerned about competing demands on an employee's time? Telework allows even greater flexibility in balancing personal and professional responsibilities, though it is not a substitute for dependent care.

How can you and your employees continue business as usual during a crisis/emergency? Telework allows working during emergency situations, which means you can fulfill your mission even during business interruptions.

Telework is most effective when tailored to the business needs of a team, and when it meets the needs of the agency, the manager, and the employee. With more than a dozen years of proven success in the federal government, telework is far beyond the experimental stage. Telework works – period. It's up to you to decide how best to adapt it to your own situation.

For Trainers:

The employees you select to telework should be self-disciplined, independent and results-driven. Employees who perform well onsite will most likely perform well no matter where they work. Before implementing your program, you will need to train your employees. You should be aware of:

☐ Your company's telework goals

☐ What makes a successful teleworker

☐ Suitable teleworker characteristics

☐ Red flags

☐ Team success factors

☐ Leveraging the technology

☐ Maximizing virtual meetings

☐ Facing the challenges

Training should include:

☐ Equipment and software

☐ Company and employee equipment liability

☐ Information security

☐ Working at home challenges

☐ How to "Get a buddy" – someone you can go to for advice

☐ Creating and organizing your workspace

☐ Staying in touch with the office

☐ Obtaining supervisor feedback

Training employees before the program is only the beginning. Ongoing training should be utilized as the program grows. Teleworkers will need to be able to:

☐ Build trust with supervisors

☐ Avoid misconceptions by coworkers

☐ Create a seamless environment for customers

☐ Plan for a productive day

☐ Avoid creating additional work for others

☐ Avoid overworking (know when and how to end the workday)

☐ Avoid procrastination

☐ Avoid potential household distractions

Identify Your Training Audiences

Training is beneficial for anyone who interacts with a teleworker, even those who aren't actually teleworking. Everyone should know the eligibility factors, processes, policy and guidelines to help manage the expectations for the program. Training everyone will ensure a smoother launch. Think about including the following in your telework training:

☐ Teleworkers

☐ Managers of teleworkers

☐ Any onsite employees who interact with teleworkers. These employees will learn effective ways of communicating with those offsite

☐ Members of your IT or technology division. Most likely, your teleworkers will rely on technology and should be trained by IT staff on all applicable policies, as well as how to access company servers, email, etc.

Tips

Hold pre-telework training sessions for all your employees. These sessions will help ensure success.

By training more than just your teleworkers, you can help integrate new business practices across the whole team. On the following pages, you will find possible pre-telework training topics for all your employees. Look through these topics and determine which are relevant for your employees. The format, structure, number, and type of sessions is up to you, as these are best determined by your company's size, culture, and how you typically handle company training.

Step Three: Organization – Getting Together a Game Plan

Discuss your organization's goals for establishing a telework program:

- ☐ Enable work anytime, anywhere
- ☐ Reduce real estate/costs
- ☐ Enhance recruiting, and retain valuable employees
- ☐ Business continuity
- ☐ Expand options for Americans With Disabilities ACT (ADA) accommodation
- ☐ Increase productivity and work quality
- ☐ Increase collaboration
- ☐ Encourage management by results
- ☐ Contribute to improved traffic congestion/air quality

Checklist

Discuss items that are in place to help ensure the telework program success:

- ☐ Policy and program well-suited to the organization
- ☐ Business focus: goals and metrics
- ☐ Administrative infrastructure
- ☐ The right technology
- ☐ Optimal support system
- ☐ Communications strategy
- ☐ Training for stakeholders

Checklist

Discuss factors that will help ensure the success of your teleworking teams:

- ☐ Communication
- ☐ Best practices
- ☐ Meetings: how, when, who
- ☐ Face time
- ☐ Sharing data, experiences
- ☐ Honesty
- ☐ Tracking and reporting
- ☐ Set goals
- ☐ Measure success

Checklist

☐ Refine

☐ Celebrate

Discuss characteristics of successful teleworkers:

Checklist
- ☐ Self-motivated, self-managing
- ☐ Results-oriented
- ☐ Conscientious, organized
- ☐ Independent worker
- ☐ Flexible
- ☐ Understands job requirements
- ☐ Understands organizational policies and procedures
- ☐ Communicates well with colleagues and clients
- ☐ Handles change well

Discuss how teleworkers will communicate with their managers and coworkers:

Checklist
- ☐ Leverage the technology
- ☐ Reach out and touch: phone, voicemail, cell phones, speakerphones
- ☐ Make email an information tool, not a communication tool
- ☐ Share space on the Intra- or Internet
- ☐ Maximize videoconferencing
- ☐ Try collaboration software tools

Maximize virtual meetings

Checklist
- ☐ Prepare and distribute agenda
- ☐ Agree upon meeting outcomes
- ☐ Propose procedures (e.g., polling, voting) and signals
- ☐ Decide on tone: formal or informal
- ☐ Agree on leadership
- ☐ Agree on ground rules
- ☐ Confirm outcomes, next steps, responsibilities
- ☐ De-brief before closing

Discuss employee concerns and other potential issues your group can foresee, and brainstorm solutions:

- ☐ What if I'm the only one in the office?
- ☐ What if more work falls on me?
- ☐ What if my backup isn't performing the way I need them to?
- ☐ What if I don't like teleworking?
- ☐ What if someone on the team isn't pulling their weight?

Checklist

For more information about pre-telework training see Appendix One. Appendixes can be found at http://governmenttraininginc.com/Managing-Teleworkers-110809.asp.

Setting up a Continuity of Operations Plan to Maintain Essential Functions

Federal operations and facilities have been disrupted by a range of events, including:

☐ The terrorist attacks on September 11, 2001, and at Oklahoma City

☐ Severe weather events, such as hurricanes Katrina, Rita, and Wilma in 2005

☐ Building-level events, such as asbestos contamination at the Department of the Interior's headquarters.

Such disruptions, particularly if prolonged, can lead to interruptions in essential government services. Prudent management, therefore, requires that federal agencies develop plans for ensuring the continuity of such services in emergency situations. These are referred to as continuity of operations (COOP) plans. These plans lay out an agency's approach to maintaining services, ensuring proper authority for government actions, and protecting vital assets.

Continuity of Operations (COOP)

The Federal Emergency Management Agency's Federal Continuity Directive (FDC) 1 defines COOP planning as "an effort within individual agencies to ensure they can continue to perform their Mission Essential Functions (MEFs) and Primary Mission Essential Functions (PMEFs) during a wide range of emergencies, including localized acts of nature, accidents, and technological or attack-related emergencies." The primary goal of continuity in the Executive branch is the continuation of essential functions." COOP is intended to be short-term; it must be functional within 12 hours and may last up to 30 days.

Federal agencies are required by Presidential Decision Directive (PDD) 67 to develop plans for ensuring the continuity of such services in emergency situations. This directive also designated the Federal Emergency Management Agency (FEMA) as lead agent for executive branch COOP planning, which includes the responsibility for formulating guidance on planning and assessing the status of executive branch COOP capabilities.

In response, FEMA issued COOP guidance to agencies in July 1999: Federal Preparedness Circular (FPC) 65. The circular states that, in order to have a viable COOP capability, agencies should identify their essential functions, which then provide the basis for subsequent planning steps. The circular further states that agencies must designate alternate facilities as part of their continuity plans and prepare their personnel for the possibility of unannounced relocation to these facilities.

In June 2004, FEMA released an updated version of FPC 65, providing additional guidance to agencies on each of the topics covered in the original guidance, including an annex on alternate facilities. According to the update, an agency must identify an alternate facility that provides sufficient space for relocated personnel to perform essential agency functions during a COOP event. Agencies are also directed to identify the levels of staff and resources required at the alternate facility to support the performance of these functions. The identification of staff and resources, including equipment, critical information systems and data, and vital records, establishes the preparation requirements for an alternate facility. For example, for an agency to determine that it has an adequate number of computers present at the alternate facility, it must first establish how many are required to support personnel in the performance of essential functions. Once critical resources are identified, pre-positioning them at an alternate facility is necessary.

Requirements

The 2004 version of FPC 65 also states that agencies should consider telework (also known as work-at-home or flexiplace) as an option in their COOP planning. Although FPC 65 does not require agency plans to incorporate telework, using this option allows employees to contribute to the performance of agency essential functions without having to physically relocate to an alternate operating facility. The following bullets categorize key areas that an agency must consider when selecting and preparing its alternate facility.

Site selection: Before an agency selects a location for its alternate facility, it should perform an all-hazard risk assessment to determine, among other things, any natural hazards that may affect the facility and its security against crime, sabotage, and terrorist attacks. When

selecting a location, an agency should consider access to essential resources, such as food, water, and fuel. Finally, the agency should be able to run emergency power at the facility.

Facility plans and procedures: An agency must have detailed site preparation and activation plans to achieve full operational capability within 12 hours of notification. An agency must have plans for notifying its alternate facility upon COOP activation of plans to relocate, for reception and in processing of COOP personnel upon arrival, and to address housing for the relocated personnel.

Employee health, safety, security, and emotional well-being: An agency must provide consideration for the health, safety, and emotional well-being of its relocating COOP personnel and ensure that physical security at the alternate facility meets all requirements established by annual threat assessments and physical security surveys.

Space: An agency should ensure that space at its alternate facility is adequate for supporting the number of relocating COOP personnel identified in the agency's staffing plans.

Equipment: An agency should identify the critical resources, including information technology and telecommunications equipment, needed to perform essential functions. An agency must pre-position critical resources at its alternate facility and have procedures for ordering any last-minute equipment.

Vital records: Agency personnel must have access to electronic and hard-copy vital records and databases to perform essential functions from the alternate facility. The agency must develop a vital records inventory and be able to access this information from the facility.

Voice and data communications: An agency must have redundant communications providing the capability to communicate with key contacts, including agency staff, critical customers, and the public. It must also provide access to a local area network, electronic vital records, critical information systems and data, and internal and external email and archives.

Tests and exercises: An agency must conduct and document tests and exercises of its COOP plans and procedures to ensure that, among other things, requirements at the alternate facility are adequate for performing essential functions.

Manager COOP Responsibilities

Understand the agency COOP plan and management roles in executing the plan.

Notify employees designated as essential personnel for COOP.

Communicate expectations both to COOP and non-COOP employees regarding steps needed in case of an emergency.

Establish communication processes to notify COOP and non-COOP employees of COOP status in the event of an emergency.

Integrate COOP expectations into telework agreements as appropriate.

In case of an emergency, allow essential personnel to telework regularly.

Telework COOP Responsibilities

Telework can play a vital role in helping agencies preserve their essential functionality in this environment and should be part of all agency emergency planning. Management must be committed to implementing remote work arrangements as broadly as possible to take full advantage of the potential of telework for this purpose, ensuring that:

☐ Equipment, technology, and technical support have been tested

☐ Employees are comfortable with technology and communications methods

☐ Managers are comfortable managing a distributed workgroup

In addition, agencies and management should consider investing in and using teleconferencing, videoconferencing, and other technologies that enable multi-channel communication, as well as paperless systems.

Additionally, teleworkers need to:

☐ Maintain a current telework agreement detailing any COOP responsibilities, as appropriate

☐ Practice telework regularly to ensure effectiveness

☐ Be familiar with agency and workgroup COOP plans and individual expectations during COOP events

Emergency Dismissal

Snow storms, large-scale road closures, demonstrations or other events that temporarily shut down portions of urban areas may necessitate closure of some federal government offices. However, the event causing the closure may not affect individuals who are or could telework on that day. Agencies may therefore require teleworkers to work when the agency is closed for these situations.

Any requirement that an employee continues to telework if the agency closes (or dismisses employees early) on his or her telework day or on any of his or her regularly scheduled work days should be included in the employee's telework agreement. Managers may excuse a telework employee from duty during an emergency situation if the emergency adversely affects the telework site (e.g., disruption of electricity, loss of heat, etc.), if the teleworker faces a personal hardship that prevents him or her from completing assigned duties, or if the teleworker must have contact with the office to work.

Pandemic Influenza

The National Strategy for Pandemic Influenza Implementation Plan references the benefits of using telework to slow the spread of disease by keeping face-to-face contact (often referred to as "social distancing") to a minimum while maintaining operations as close to normal as possible. Telework can also help agencies retain functionality, as infrastructure issues and other challenges make the main work site difficult to access.

The key to successful use of telework in the event of a pandemic health crisis is an effective routine program. As many employees as possible should have telework capability – current telework arrangements, connectivity, and equipment commensurate with their work needs, and frequent enough opportunities to telework to ensure all systems have been tested and are known to be functional. This may entail creative thinking as to how to implement telework, drawing in employees who otherwise might not engage in remote access, and ensuring their effectiveness as a distributed workforce.

Manager Pandemic Responsibilities

Implement telework to the greatest extent possible in the workgroup, so systems are in place to support successful remote work in an emergency.

Communicate expectations to all employees regarding their roles and responsibilities in relation to remote work in the event of a pandemic health crisis.

Establish communication processes to notify employees of activation of the plan.

Integrate pandemic health crisis response expectations into telework agreements.

With the employee, assess requirements for working at home (supplies and equipment needed for an extended telework period).

Determine how all teleworkers will communicate with one another and with management.

Identify how time and attendance will be maintained.

Teleworker Pandemic Responsibilities

Update current telework agreement to specifying pandemic health crisis responsibilities, as appropriate.

Perform all duties assigned by management, even if they are outside usual or customary requirements.

Practice telework regularly to ensure effectiveness.

Be familiar with agency and workgroup plans and individual expectations for telework during a pandemic health crisis.

Step Four: Implementation – Setting and Maintaining Standards

Managing by Results

Performance management can be applied to all employees, both onsite and off and involves two distinct operations. First, specify attainable work objectives and standards for employees so that they know:

- ☐ What must be done?
- ☐ Why it must be done.
- ☐ How well it must be done.
- ☐ By when it must be done.
- ☐ What constitutes a job that is complete?

Ask yourself, "What will it take in that teleworker's performance to put a smile on my face?" In other words: "How will I know a fully satisfactory end product if I see it?" Finding the right answer minimizes the chance that your teleworkers will waste time and resources going after the wrong objectives. Also, the more clear the initial description of objectives, the better you and your teleworker will cope with the reduction or absence of informal hallway encounters where you might discuss and fine-tune those expectations.

The second part of performance management involves reviewing performance and giving feedback. Your teleworkers aren't mind readers; be clear with them about your expectations for their performance. Follow these feedback guidelines:

- ☐ Be descriptive about what the person did ("You have three mistakes in the budget for the next quarter."), and don't use subjective labels ("This is sloppy work.").
- ☐ Limit feedback to priority changes. Don't try to fix everything at once, but begin with the changes that will account for the most improvement and value.
- ☐ Give feedback sooner rather than later. The employee might make the same mistake over and over again until he hears otherwise, so provide feedback quickly.

☐ Give positive and negative feedback. Describe what needs to be changed, but also discuss what's being done well. That way the person can continue along the right path and be recognized for a job well done.

☐ "Praise in public, criticize in private." Everyone likes to hear good news about what they've done well in front of peers, but the negative feedback should remain between worker and manager.

Remember that the key is to focus on the final product, not the processes used to develop it.

Remember

Keeping Track of the Telework Operation

Clarify in your own mind how telework will help your group's operations and results.

When done well, telework benefits everyone: employees, the agency, and the public. The first step in assuring this happens for you, the manager, is to determine how telework can be used as a business solution to business problems. Telework done solely in response to employee requests or direction from top management is not likely to lead to observable, sustained results. Managers who find ways to link telework to the kinds of problems they themselves face (e.g., deadline pressures, staff turnover, space limitations) are most likely to use telework in ways that make sense for everyone involved. Similarly, schedules for all teleworkers in your group need not be the same. In fact, you will want to make them deliberately different to ensure adequate coverage in the office.

Be specific to ensure understanding about your expectations.

Tell teleworkers what is expected of them in terms of work procedures. For example, depending on your circumstances you may want to specify how they should inform coworkers and customers about their work schedules or how often, if at all, they should check in or how often they should check their voicemail and email, etc. As with any kind of work arrangement, ensure there is a clear mutual understanding of and agreement on work assignments, expected products, and timeframes. One big difference between telework and office-based work is that telework removes many of the opportunities for casual encounters where work goals and progress can be discussed "on the fly." Those casual meetings are replaced in telework by more deliberated, planned discussions in advance, to clarify expectations and head off performance problems. This is one example of how the manager of teleworkers invariably starts adopting or making more use of fundamental management techniques that often fall into disuse in the typical office setting.

Maintain equitable expectations and performance standards for telework.

Although working at home or at a telework center may allow teleworkers to get work done with fewer distractions, this does not mean that you should assign them more work or change your expectations or their performance standards. Avoid assigning teleworkers more or less work than you normally would if they were in the office. Telework does not change an employee's job responsibilities. It just changes where the work gets done. However, if you do notice that a teleworker has been able to produce more or better work (as is often the case), be sure to compliment him/her so the teleworker won't feel that extra effort is taken for granted.

Establish effective communication techniques for staying in touch with teleworkers and for enabling/encouraging them to stay in touch with coworkers and customers.

As with most work situations, effective communication is an asset. When working with a teleworker, you may need to change your typical communication techniques and circumstances. You will probably find that you start relying more on a mix of face-to-face conversations, live phone calls, voicemail, email, and audio and/or Web conferencing. Update yourself on the techniques and technology available to facilitate and maintain effective and convenient communication with your teleworking staff. Encourage and facilitate ongoing communications between teleworkers and their in-office peers and customers. Those coworkers and customers should feel it is just as easy to have access to and get a response from a teleworker as an office worker. Keep in mind, however, that no manager has 100-percent access to his/her staff all of the time even if they all work in the office. People are away from their desks for many reasons (e.g., meetings, meals, travel, sick days, breaks), and it's a myth that managers necessarily have less access to teleworkers.

Establish clear procedures for handling customer inquiries.

Customers need not know if someone is in the office or teleworking. Customer calls to the office should be transferred directly to your teleworkers regardless of where they are working. This may require some telecommunications support. Teleworkers should handle customer questions just as if they were in the office. Never tell customers their request cannot be fulfilled because "John/Mary is working at home today." Work out a plan with your teleworkers for responding to these situations.

Reinforce the fact that telework will not add to the duties of office workers.

Your regular office workers may be concerned about fairness and equity in work assignments. A particular concern is how unexpected, short-fuse situations will be handled. It may seem easier to turn to the staff member who is close at hand for these urgent

assignments. However, you may want to stop and think about who is best qualified for the assignment – and that might be the teleworker who is only as far away as a phone call. One determinant of how many teleworkers you will approve in your group, and how many days each will telework, is this issue of ensuring fairness and equity. Telework can be a destructive work practice if the performance and satisfaction of the teleworkers goes up at the expense of their in-office peers.

Reassure employees who are in the office every day that they will not be expected to undertake job assignments that would normally go to the teleworker. Once you have clarified that, take care to avoid assigning them such duties. Part of your planning for telework should include a meeting with the entire work group to think through how teleworking might affect normal workflow and movement of documents, and then brainstorm with the group how to develop new solutions that incorporate telework.

Discuss and identify which tasks are suitable for telework.

Portable tasks are generally amenable for telework. Identification of such tasks is an easy and logical process, rarely if ever requiring an analysis of the job. In fact, in many cases, the teleworker can make the determination as needed and the manager simply focuses on results. If telework is new to your organization, it may be helpful to have general and/or individual discussions with your staff regarding tasks that need to be performed in the main office and those that can be completed at an alternate work site.

Remember In today's information-based workforce, most jobs contain at least some portable tasks. To the extent possible, determination of telework amenable tasks should be based on actual performance factors and not manager or teleworker personal whim. Keep an open mind. With today's technology and job content, even federal occupations that have typically had low telework numbers, such as managers and support staff, can telework effectively. Finally, ensure an open discussion and understanding of this topic for your entire staff.

Clarify procedures for discussing telework problems and, if necessary, requiring the employee to suspend or stop teleworking.

No No No matter how well you plan for telework and how much you and your employees want it to succeed, at times, a teleworker's performance becomes unacceptable. You should no more accept that from a teleworker than you would for an office worker; allowing unsatisfactory performance and results amounts to your tacit approval and encouragement of substandard work.

Performance problems may not be due to the telework itself. Make it clear to your teleworkers when they begin that you will be focusing on their work results, and if those results begin to slip you will address them as you would if they were still full-time office

workers – by confronting and analyzing the problem to determine its causes, not jumping to conclusions. Your teleworkers should know that their ability to continue in that role depends on meeting your performance expectations.

If their performance becomes substandard, work with them to uncover causes and to implement a solution, perhaps with some coaching, training, additional feedback, etc. If the problems continue, you have the right and the responsibility to require the person to suspend his telework and return to the office. If acceptable performance as a teleworker cannot be sustained, then the telework arrangement is unsuitable for that employee. Making this process clear at the outset can avoid unpleasant confrontations later, especially if the employee believes that telework is a permanent privilege.

Remember

Importance of Mentoring

A mentor is someone who shares their knowledge, wisdom, and experience about their occupation or workplace. You may have had one or more mentors during your career. In a traditional office, the mentee (one being mentored) is often a younger, less experienced version of yourself whom you feel holds great promise. However, as with most things in telecommuting, mentoring takes on a bit of different spin, focusing less on job skills and more on work environment and personal circumstances.

Rather than the manager herself, it's often more practical to have experienced telecommuting employees mentor the newcomers. You can help foster these kinds of relationships by matching up people with similar experiences, job responsibilities, and work situations. Such relationships can also develop naturally during the training period when workers start to form their own network of friends and advisors. Either way, they help strengthen morale and keep up team motivation.

Whether in or out of the office, with managers or more experienced employees, mentoring should be done with an eye to the following:

☐ Provide guidance based on past business experiences.

☐ Create a positive counseling relationship and climate of open communication.

☐ Help protégé identify problems and solutions.

☐ Lead protégé through problem-solving processes.

☐ Offer constructive criticism in a supportive way.

☐ Share stories, including mistakes.

☐ Assign "homework" if applicable.

☐ Refer protégé to other business associates.

☐ Be honest about business expertise.

☐ Solicit feedback from protégé.

☐ Come prepared to each meeting to discuss issues.

Source: Small Business Administration.

Distance Coaching

Getting and giving feedback has already been discussed; this applies to performance reviews, as well. Rather than making these a once-a-year event fraught with dread and unpleasant surprises, it's better for all concerned to regularly evaluate team members monthly or every six weeks. Yes, it takes more time, especially in the beginning, but once again the payoff will be worth it in terms of improved communication and performance. Instead of thinking "Uh-oh, what have I done this time?" when they are called on the carpet either physically or virtually, employees will hopefully approach such conversations with at least a neutral mind-set.

Current management-speak has replaced the word "counseling" with the more user-friendly and objective term "coaching." Rather than trying to "counsel" by fixing bad behavior or solving a problem, coaching implies enhancing or developing performance which sets a more positive stage for improvement. For example, call center employees at the ARO call center are evaluated using a "squeaky wheel" approach; that is, those making the most "noise" in terms of poor performance ratings on their monitored calls get the most "grease" – personal attention to improve their work performance and habits. They need to improve to a certain score to get to "maintenance" mode. Managers must be able to work with employees in this manner; each quarter, they are also assessed on the success of these efforts.

Coaching from a distance has its own particular challenges. Coaching in general implies the need for specifying goals and measurement of performance, and if you're doing it virtually these should be crystal clear since telecommuters are working independently, making many of their own decisions and solving problems.

Kimball Fisher and Maureen Duncan Fisher, authors of The Distance Manager, suggest a proactive approach to coaching. By coaching proactively, you are dealing with situations throughout the entire project and not just when a problem arises. Proactive coaching involves what they call "on-the-spot" coaching during telephone and videoconferences or through emails. By asking open-ended questions, team members can "think through all aspects of the project and its outcome."

Similarly, a postmortem at the end of the project "provides a good opportunity to reflect on well-dones and opportunities for improvements" for future efforts. However, if the situation calls for corrective feedback, then one-on-one coaching should take place privately with the team member to avoid shaming or embarrassing him in front of his peers.

Following are some tips for distance coaching.

Listen carefully to subtleties and nuances: How do workers react to your suggestions over the phone? Is there a stone-cold silence or murmurs of agreement? If coaching is done by email, is the tone of their response defensive or appreciative? Even if you sense there's a problem or the employee seems to be struggling with a certain aspect of the job, asking an up-front question can head it off at the pass and provide a quick resolution. Coaching by email can be almost impossible as tone and wordage can often be misinterpreted. So, if you get even a whiff of dissention from an email, pick up the phone.

Implement a peer feedback process: This can be especially helpful if the manager is far removed from the employees. Often team members work more closely with one another and are, therefore, more familiar with processes and problems. However, such a system needs to be implemented equally for everyone, using what the Fishers describe as a "stop/start/continue" method that specifies behaviors that need to be changed (stopped), modified (started), and praised (continued). "Having peers give input provides a more balanced and accurate picture," say the authors. However, it must take place in a supportive, constructive and nonthreatening atmosphere.

Utilize one-on-one coaching: As mentioned earlier, this does require more time, but since neither you (nor anyone else) is a mind reader, it allows you to catch problems at the beginning, stay informed as to exactly what's happening, and maintain a positive and open relationship with workers. It also builds loyalty and can "move the coaching process in the arena of developmental conversations versus coaching only when problems arise." See the following for a suggested format for individual coaching sessions.

Telecommuter One-on-One Coaching Format

Team Member Name: Date:

Update on personal development plan:

Discussion of key projects (deadlines, issues, problems, etc.):

Business information for team member:

Feedback on team member performance (well-dones, areas for improvement, etc.):

Source: The Distance Manager, by Kimball Fisher and Maurine Duncan Fisher. New York: McGraw-Hill, p.70.

Develop a structured improvement plan when the situation warrants. The employee can put it together. But "be clear about expectations and set boundaries for what needs to be included … keep[ing] responsibility for success with the individual," state Fisher and Fisher. By investing effort in his own success, the employee is more likely to internalize improvements and changes.

Spotting Potential Problems

No No

Say you've tried everything: Listened to their concerns and ideas, shared information, been available, provided encouragement and recognition, and so forth, and the telecommuting arrangement doesn't seem to be working out. This could be due to several factors.

The job responsibilities are not suited to telework. If the employee finds that she's needed in the office more often than not and spends much less time working at home than in the office, the arrangement needs to be re-evaluated.

The employee is not familiar enough with the organization or the job to work independently from home. He may need time to get his "sea legs" under the closer supervision of the office, and you may also need to become more acquainted with the kind and quality of his work to see if it even will benefit from telecommuting. The telecommuting arrangement can be put on hold until the desired level of competence and confidence is reached by all concerned.

The individual lacks the "telecommuting personality;" that is, the characteristics necessary for telework discussed earlier. Not everyone is suited for telecommuting – in fact, once they get into it, they may find it lonely and counterproductive. The worker may need to return to the office or may not be suited to the job at all.

Regardless of the cause, if productivity or customer service starts to suffer at any point during the telecommuting arrangement, then you as a manager need to take immediate action. The longer you wait, the worse it will likely get.

Management requires fairness and objectivity, as well as an ability to communicate effectively, analyze causes, and determine workable solutions. Few people, if any, enjoy telling someone they are screwing up. In fact, some managers go to great lengths to avoid such discussions, instead dealing with problems indirectly or in a passive aggressive manner. In an office, this usually manifests itself when the unsuspecting worker finds she has fewer assignments, is excluded from meetings, or that her desk has been moved to a less pleasant area after a few days away. That is so much easier than a face-to-face confrontation!

Not really, especially with telecommuters. Not only will the burden of work fall more heavily on the rest of the team, creating an unfair situation and setup for resentment, but the individual will still be getting paid the same for doing less, draining the resources of the company and being counterproductive to its goals.

Rather, you might want to view the situation as an opportunity for coaching the worker and helping him improve, even if he has to return to the office or go for additional training. So, if a problem becomes apparent – or even hints at surfacing – deal with it immediately and directly.

What Happens When Things Don't Work Out?

Despite everyone's best intentions and careful planning, problems may arise in telework arrangements. As with any performance problem, you should respond in a constructive and timely manner. You may want to call the employee into the office for a face-to-face meeting to discuss your concerns and the specific problems. You may need to clarify that their ability to telework depends upon whether they can turn the situation around.

Make sure you listen carefully to the employee's side of the story. The end result should be that the conversation is both solution- and results-oriented. Solutions may include:

- ☐ Rescinding the telework arrangement
- ☐ Modifying the telework agreement to better define your expectations
- ☐ Setting a timeframe for the employee to demonstrate a significant improvement
- ☐ Resolving other circumstances that may have contributed to the unsatisfactory performance

Setting up the Home Office

Getting Organized in a Remote Setting

Become familiar with office technology guidelines. When working from home or another telework location, you should know when and how to logon to your agency's server, what logins and passwords to use, and what information is security sensitive. Depending on your circumstances, there may be other important factors to cover/learn regarding telework technology and remote access. Obtain the necessary guidance, training, manuals, and contact information for effective use and troubleshooting of your technology. Your information technology office telework program manual, and/or telework coordinator are good sources for information. Given the challenges associated with remote troubleshooting and technical support, you may even want to develop some minimal troubleshooting skills of your own.

Tips

Set up a home workspace or make arrangements to work at a telework center. Your workspace, whether located in your home, a telework center, or other alternate work site, should be arranged for maximum comfort and performance. Consider factors, such as the lighting, noise levels, and furniture. Make sure there are no safety hazards in your home office, such as wires in walkways, loose rugs, unstable furniture, or overloaded electrical outlets. OPM, GSA, and Department of Labor Websites (among others) contain abundant information and guidance on setting up workstations. Check the guidance from your own organization.

Your telework coordinator can provide information about available telework centers and the procedures for registering to use one. You can also obtain telework center information from the telework center Website: http://www.gsa.gov/Portal/gsa/ep/contentView.do? bodyOnly=true&contentId=24053&contentType=GSA_BASIC. Visit the center before committing to use it as your telework location. Is it really more convenient than your main office? Is there adequate secure parking? Will you be able to leave work materials there overnight? Is it accessible during the hours you need? Does it have the equipment, furniture, and workstation arrangement that you want/need?

Be flexible in your telework schedule. Because circumstances can change, your telework schedule should be flexible enough to address changes in work requirements. For example, there's a meeting in the office on a day you normally telework, you may need to switch telework days to attend the meeting. Remember, the telework arrangement should work both for the employee and management.

Remember Prepare to work in your home. Working at home, even if it is only one day a week, represents a change from the traditional office. Before you start, think about exactly how you want to set up your workspace. Keep in mind that many of the considerations for working at home may also apply to working at a telework center or any alternative work location. Identify a suitable work location that includes the items listed below.

Adequate Work Space

Find a space at home that supports work-related activities. If you telework on a regular basis, this will probably involve dedicating a room or part of a room to job-related activities. Depending on your assignments, the setting may need to be large enough to accommodate a computer, printer, fax machine, files, and storage shelves. In other instances, you may only need a worktable, comfortable chair, and a phone. If you have young children or pets at home, you will have to protect your files and equipment. For the sake of comfort and efficiency, locate all of your office equipment in the same area with your workstation.

Control Over Lighting and Sound

Proper lighting is vital for avoiding eyestrain and maximizing efficient performance. When writing or reading, you should have ample lighting. If you are using a computer, be aware of the light levels in your work area. Too much light or light striking the screen at the wrong angle can cause glare, resulting in eyestrain and fatigue. Non-glare filters over the monitor screen may diminish fatigue. Shield your workspace from household noise and the household from work-related noise. Various ways of soundproofing your environment include locating your office in a room at the farthest point from the TV room or kitchen (this could include a basement or, if feasible and practical, a detached garage); having the area professionally soundproofed or doing it yourself; or at the very least, closing the door. Where applicable, you and other members of the household may need to figure out ways to facilitate your teleworking and the activity of other household members without disturbing each other.

Access to Telephone and Electrical Outlets

For jobs requiring a computer, a grounded power outlet is essential. Surge protection devices between the electrical outlet and computer protect equipment from voltage spikes. A "work" telephone line may be necessary to support work-related phone calls and faxes.

Equipment Needs, Computers and Email

The following information can also be distributed in leaflet form by the manager to prospective teleworkers. It details what equipment is needed by the teleworker and will help determine what has to be ordered and installed, as well as what software and training might be required.

Computers and Connectivity

The manager and IT department must know what operating system will be used and how the teleworker will connect to the Internet – wireless or DSL. Obviously, the closer the teleworker's home equipment matches the technology capabilities of the office the easier it will be to ensure full compatibility.

Telephone and Voicemail

The teleworker will need a telephone line and voicemail system for calling and receiving messages from the manager, coworkers, and customers. For part-time or occasional teleworkers, an ideal solution provides automatic forwarding of incoming calls to the remote telephone and remote access to the office voicemail system. If you are a full-time teleworker, you may not need an office telephone extension at all.

Dedicated Phone Line/DSL/Cable Modem

The teleworker will need to be able to talk on the telephone and check email at the same time. This will require wireless capability, DSL or cable-modem Internet connection. Depending on the nature of the job, you may need high-speed Internet to download large files.

Printer

Printer requirements vary with the nature of the job. In some cases, teleworkers may be able to email the occasional document to the office for printing or wait until they are back in the office to print it. In other instances, they will need printing capability at their telework site. Never rely on coworkers to routinely print out documents from email.

Fax Machine

Thanks to email and other forms of electronic communication, fax machines are not as necessary as they used to be. However, they can be helpful if actual signatures are needed or if a paper document needs to be reviewed.

Cell Phones

Cell phones, particularly BlackBerries, iPhones, and other PDAs provide both long-distance calling and immediate Internet access. Depending upon its policy, the organization may reimburse all or part of these expenses.

Tips Work with your teleworkers to determine what technology requirements they need and agree on a plan for installing, maintaining, and setting up the technology. Be sure to address the following topics in your discussions:

☐ Equipment acquisition

☐ Equipment installation

☐ Equipment maintenance and repair

☐ Software requirements and standards

☐ Virus protection

☐ Remote access and dial-in procedures

☐ Equipment and data security

☐ Data storage and backups

☐ Compatibility with office technology

Step Four: Implementation – Setting and Maintaining Standards

Safety and Working from Home

When working from home, teleworkers must address issues of personal safety. This is not relevant to telework centers, where appropriate workstations are provided.

Government employees causing or suffering work-related injuries and/or damages at the alternative work site (home, telework center, or other location) are covered by the Military Personnel and Civilian Employees Claims Act, the Federal Tort Claims Act, or the Federal Employees' Compensation Act (workers' compensation), as appropriate.

Manager Safety Responsibilities

Review safety checklist with teleworker.

Depending on agency policy, managers may have the authority to visit home offices, with advance notice to the teleworker.

Teleworker Safety Responsibilities (for home-based telework)

Provide appropriate telework space, with ergonomically correct chair, desk, and computer equipment.

Complete safety checklist certifying the space as free from hazards. This checklist is not legally binding, but details management expectations and, if signed, assumes compliance.

Immediately report any work-related accident occurring at the telework site and provide the supervisor with all medical documentation related to the accident. An agency representative may need to access the home office to investigate the accident.

Lighting

Good lighting in your home office is important to reduce eyestrain. Here are some lighting suggestions:

☐ Make sure lighting isn't too bright.

☐ Avoid white reflective furniture.

☐ If you are using a desk lamp, choose a low wattage light bulb. Direct the light toward papers, not eyes.

☐ Use blinds or drapes to eliminate outdoor light.

☐ Avoid bright lighting on your monitor.

Monitor

☐ Adjust the monitor so that the screen is slightly below eye level.

☐ Position the monitor to minimize glare.

☐ Clean the screen on a regular basis.

Checklist

☐ Position yourself about 20"-24" away from the monitor.

☐ Center your monitor on the user.

☐ Keep your head at a comfortable level.

Safety hazards

Remember Whether you work from a home or remote office, work spaces are often full of dangers that threaten the physical well-being of all who enter. Company coworkers or, at home, family members and pets can unknowingly be in harm's way. While some threats are fairly obvious, others can lurk in the most unexpected places.

Office cables and wires are far more than an unsightly nuisance. Slips, trips and falls constitute the majority of general industry accidents. They cause 15 percent of all accidental, job-related deaths and are second only to motor vehicles as a cause of fatalities, according to the Occupational Safety and Health Administration (OSHA). Therefore, keep power adaptors, modems, power strips, hubs, and so on, off the floor. Don't overload electrical outlets and always have a fire extinguisher on hand. Check it at regular intervals to ensure it is still functional. Also make sure filing cabinets and tall bookcases are anchored to the wall, so they can't topple over.

Home Office Ergonomics

More than five million Americans or 3.8 percent of our population work from home. Whether it's telecommuting or starting a home-based business, Americans are spending more time in home offices that are not ergonomically equipped. The result is more back and neck pain from poorly designed chairs and workspaces and more headaches and eye strain from bad lighting.

"Most people don't give one thought to the chair they are sitting in while they work, yet they will spend years of their lives molded to that piece of furniture," said Mark McLaughlin, MD, of Princeton Brain and Spine Care. "A well-balanced, ergonomic chair at work is one of the best preventative interventions one can do for the spine. It could prevent many episodes of back and neck pain flare-ups and, in some settings, even help prevent spine surgery."

Chair

Tips Your chair is the most important piece of furniture in your office. You want to find a comfortable chair that has the following characteristics:

☐ Adjustable height

☐ Lower, raise, and tilt backwards

☐ 16" to 20" off of the floor

☐ Lumbar support

☐ Good backrest and wide enough to support shoulders

☐ Chair's seat should allow 1"-4" of space between edge of chair and your knees

☐ Front edge of seat is curved

☐ Five wheels

☐ Padded armrests that can lower or raise

Before you purchase your chair, make sure to give it a test drive. If possible, move the chair that you like in front of a desk and see how it feels. Adjust the seat so that your feet are flat on the floor. When you do this, the lumbar support should fit into the small of your back. The chair should fit your body and meet the above-stated guidelines. Although a good chair that is already assembled can cost anywhere from $400 - $2,000, you can get a similar model for much less, provided you're willing to take the time to put it together. Most office supply store will have several models to "test drive" and select from before making a final purchase.

Desk

Before purchasing a desk, evaluate your needs. What is your profession? What equipment will you be using? How much desktop room will you need? Make sure to allow space for computer equipment, telephone, Rolodex, other office supplies, and writing room. You also need room for heavily used items on your desk, or you might have to constantly stretch, twist, and turn to reach things. You can also use height-adjustable large tables which are cost effective. These tables let you move from keyboard to side table without having to hunch your shoulders.

Keyboard and Mouse

Since it is so important to have your wrists at the right height when using input devices, a tray system is important to consider as an option. Choose a system that has the following features:

☐ Height adjustable

☐ Adjustable angle

☐ Allows for upper arm relaxation by right angle position of arms

The keyboard should be 28"-30" off of the floor. If your keyboard is too low, you will slump over it, and if it is too high, you will strain your wrists. A good keyboard will not flatten your hands and bend your wrists; keyboards that are split and/or tilt may be better than the traditional flat model.

A wrist pad for the front of your keyboard will also cushion your wrists.

A computer mouse can cause the hand to twist into uncomfortable positions, resulting in wrist injuries. Try to use the mouse with a sweeping movement, instead of a quick, twisting motion. Use your mouse as little as possible or purchase a trackball instead. Trackballs allow for programming a lock button, omitting the need to click and drag.

Posture

Tips

Although it can be easy to forget about when in the middle of working, take the time to learn how to sit properly, doing the following:

- ☐ Relax shoulders
- ☐ Wrists straight
- ☐ Back in contact with lumbar support of your chair
- ☐ Legs in contact with your seat
- ☐ Feet on the floor
- ☐ Elbows at a right angle when typing
- ☐ Upper arm and elbow close to body
- ☐ Head and neck straight

If you find yourself slumping over, practice good posture while doing a routine activity, such as watching TV or driving a car. Even being aware that you need to sit up straight can help correct posture and avoid a myriad of problems that can result strain on shoulders, neck, and back.

Home Inspection

To home inspect or not to home inspects seems a major point of controversy among managers. The following are some pros and cons regarding home inspections.

From the Telework Exchange:

Q: My organization (I'm a fed) just established a telework directive. As part of the process for approving telework from home, the supervisor is required to inspect the home office for

compliance with government safety standards. This seems extreme to me. Is it normal to require home office inspections as a pre-condition to telework?

A: No, it is not a typical government policy or practice. According to information found in the federal government's telework Website (www.telework.gov), "the agency is not required to visit the teleworker's home to inspect it for safety and ergonomics."

In fact, a requirement for supervisors to inspect home offices should be discouraged. Why? Primarily, because your supervisor is unlikely to be a safety specialist with sufficient knowledge of Occupational Safety and Health (OSHA) rules and regulations to make an informed decision about your home office setup.

A formal approval by your supervisor, as the government's representative, means that the government has agreed that your home office meets all applicable regulations. This requirement creates greater liability for your agency and could result in supervisors being more reluctant to approve telework requests. After all, how many supervisors would care to be put in this position, in addition to dealing with the logistics involved in carrying out home office inspections?

There is a better alternative. Many agencies use a "Self-Certification" Safety Checklist, which requires the employee to review their home office against listed OSHA standards and certify that it is compliant. This meets the goal of encouraging a focus on safety without creating a liability for managers. Agencies still reserve the right to inspect home offices, with advance notice, if a concern exists about safety or security issues.

Source: http://www.teleworkexchange.com/teleworker-03-09g.asp

From HrHero.com:

The Occupational Safety and Health Administration (OSHA) does not have any regulations governing telework in home offices. The agency issued a directive in February 2000 stating that it won't conduct inspections of employees' home offices, won't hold employers liable for employees' home offices, and doesn't expect employers to inspect their employees' home offices. (See OSHA Directive CPL 2-0.125 for more information.)

OSHA conducts inspections of other home-based work sites, such as "home manufacturing operations," only when it receives a complaint or referral that indicates a violation of a safety or health standard that threatens physical harm or that an imminent danger exists, including reports of a work-related fatality. The scope of the inspection in an employee's home will be limited to his work activities. Note, however, that the OSHA directive deems employers responsible for home work sites if there are hazards caused by

materials, equipment, or work processes that the employer provides or requires to be used in an employee's home.

Source: http://hrhero.com/hl/articles/2009/09/18/telecommuting-tips-for-managing-employees-who-work-from-home/

According to the Office of Personnel Management (OPM) agencies should make sure that the telework employee's work site meets acceptable standards. One option is to have employees complete a self-certification safety inspection form. Onsite inspections, with adequate notice to the employee, are another option.

The following is a workspace safety checklist from the Defense Finance and Accounting Service (DFAS) that can be used as a self-certification checklist, or can be completed by the supervisor, team leader, or other designated inspector.

WORKSTATION INSPECTION/SAFETY SELF-CERTIFICATION CHECKLIST FOR HOME-BASED TELECOMMUTERS

PRIVACY ACT STATEMENT AUTHORITY: Public Law 106-346, Section 359, dated October 23, 2000. PRINCIPAL PURPOSE(S): Information on this form will be used to determine the eligibility of an employee to participate in the Defense Finance and Accounting Service (DFAS) Telecommuting Program, and to communicate requirements of the program to the employee. ROUTINE USE(S): Information on this form may be disclosed to DFAS Human Resources officials, the Department of Defense, and Office of Personnel Management. It may also be used for any of the routine uses as published in the OPM/Govt 1 systems notice. DISCLOSURE: Voluntary, however, failure to complete the form may result in ineligibility for program participation.

NAME	OFFICE SYMBOL	
DUTY STATION ADDRESS		
BUSINESS TELEPHONE	TELECOMMUTING COORDINATOR	

ALTERNATE DUTY STATION ADDRESS: DESCRIBE THE DESIGNATED WORK AREA AT THE ALTERNATE DUTY STATION DESIGNATED TOUR OF OFFICIAL DUTY CHECKLIST

The following checklist is designed to assess the overall safety of the alternate duty station. This checklist can be used as a self-certification checklist, or can be completed by the supervisor, team leader, or other designated inspector.

I.   WORKPLACE ENVIRONMENT

1. Are temperature, noise, ventilation, and lighting levels adequate for maintaining employee's normal level of job performance? YES   NO

2. Are all stairs with four (4) or more steps equipped with handrails? YES   NO

3. Are all circuit breakers and/or fuses in the electrical panel labeled as to intended service? YES   NO

4. Do circuit breakers clearly indicate if they are in the open or closed position? YES   NO

5. Is all of the electrical equipment free of recognized hazards that would cause physical harm? (Frayed wires, bare conductors, loose wires, flexible wires running through walls, exposed wires to the ceiling, etc.)   YES   NO

6. Will the building's electrical system permit the grounding of electrical equipment? YES   NO

7. Are aisles, doorways, and corners free of obstructions to permit visibility and movement? YES   NO

8. Are file cabinets and storage closets arranged so drawers and doors do not open into walkways?   YES   NO

9. Do chairs have any loose casters (wheels) and are the rungs and legs of chairs sturdy? YES   NO

10. Are the phone lines, electrical cords, and extension wires secured under a desk or alongside a baseboard? YES   NO

11. Is the office space neat, clean, and free of excessive amounts of combustibles? YES   NO

12. Are floor surfaces clean, dry, level, and free of worn or frayed seams? YES   NO

13. Are carpets well secured to the floor and free of frayed or worn seams? YES   NO

14. Is there enough light for reading? YES   NO

II.   COMPUTER WORKSTATION

1. Is the chair comfortable? YES   NO

2. Does the employee know how to adjust the chair? YES   NO

3. Is the employee's back adequately supported by a backrest? YES   NO

4. When seated are the employee's feet on the floor or a footrest and are the thighs parallel with the floor? YES   NO

5. Is the employee satisfied with the placement of the screen and keyboard? YES   NO

6. Is it easy to read the text on the screen? YES   NO

7. Does the employee need a document holder? YES   NO

8. Does the employee have enough legroom at the desk? YES   NO

9. Is the screen free from noticeable glare? YES   NO

10. Is the top of the screen paralleled with or slightly above a level gaze when the employee is seated? YES   NO

11. Is there space to rest the arms while not keying? YES   NO

12. When keying, are the forearms parallel with the floor? YES   NO

13. When using the keyboard, is the employee's wrist posture neutral when keying? YES   NO

14. When using the mouse, is excessive reach and arm extension avoided? YES   NO

15. If you answer No to any of these questions, you are required to see the Safety Officer before the Telecommuting Agreement is signed.

TELECOMMUTER SIGNATURE	DATE (MM/DD/YYYY)
TELECOMMUTER EMPLOYEES MUST PROVIDE THEIR SUPERVISORS A SIGNED COPY OF THIS FORM BEFORE THEY BEGIN TO TELECOMMUTE. SUPERVISORS WILL PROVIDE COPIES OF THE FORM TO THEIR TELECOMMUTING COORDINATOR AND SAFETY OFFICE.	

DFAS Form 1402, AUG 02 (EF)

Implementing Technology Requirements

Consult with your telework coordinator and information technology staff to help determine your agency's policies and procedures for acquiring, installing, and maintaining technology. There should be a coordinated effort among managers and staff so that technology requirements are planned for and, in turn, implemented efficiently and effectively.

Consider these areas when developing a plan to provide telework technology:

☐ Equipment acquisition

☐ Equipment installation

☐ Equipment maintenance and repair

☐ Software requirements and standards

☐ Virus protection

☐ Remote access procedures

☐ Help desk and technical support

☐ Equipment and data security

☐ Data storage and backups

☐ Compatibility with office technology

Telework PCs

!
Must Do

Technology and security go hand-in-hand. One of the most important security measures for a telework PC is having a properly configured personal firewall installed and enabled. Personal firewalls are needed to stop network-based threats in many environments. If a personal firewall has a single policy for all environments, then it is likely to be too restrictive at times, such as when on the organization's internal network, and not restrictive enough at other times, such as when on a third-party external wireless network. So, personal firewalls capable of supporting multiple policies should be used whenever possible and configured properly for the enterprise environment and an external environment, at a minimum.

Security

Federal employees and their managers are responsible for the security of federal government property and information, regardless of their work location. Agency security policies do not change and should be enforced at the same rigorous level when employees telework as when they are in the office.

The Federal Information Security Management Act of 2002 (FISMA) defines information security as protecting information and information systems from unauthorized access, use, disclosure, disruption, modification, or destruction in order to provide:

Integrity, guarding against improper information modification or destruction, ensuring authenticity of all data, documents, and signatures

Confidentiality, preserving authorized restrictions on access and disclosure, including means for protecting personal privacy and proprietary information

Availability, ensuring timely and reliable access to and use of information

As in the main office, security measures should cover not only information systems and technology, but all aspects of the information systems used by the employee, including paper files, other media, storage devices, and telecommunications equipment (e.g., laptops, PDAs, and cell phones). Employees who telework from home need to keep government property and information safe, secure, and separated from their personal property and information.

Agencies managing or operating records systems are required by the Privacy Act of 1974 and other relevant laws and regulations to issue rules for maintaining the security of information contained in those records, whether in electronic or paper form. Managers and employees must follow these rules whenever they are accessing this information, whether they are working from home, at another remote location, or at their regular duty station. For example, OPM regulates access and use of government personnel records as follows:

Section 293.106(a) of title 5, Code of Federal Regulations, mandates that "all persons whose official duties require access to and use of personnel records be responsible and accountable for safeguarding those records and for ensuring that the records are secured whenever they are not in use or under the direct control of authorized persons. Generally, personnel records should be held, processed, or stored only where facilities and conditions are adequate to prevent unauthorized access."

Under 5 CFR 293.108, "Office and agency employees whose official duties involve personnel records shall be sensitive to individual rights to personal privacy and shall not

disclose information from any personnel record unless disclosure is part of their official duties or required by executive order, regulation, or statute (e.g., required by the Freedom of Information Act, 5 U.S.C. 552)." Also, "any Office or agency employee who makes a disclosure of personnel records knowing that such disclosure is unauthorized, or otherwise knowingly violates these regulations, shall be subject to disciplinary action and may also be subject to criminal penalties where the records are subject to the Privacy Act (5 U.S.C. 552a)."

Each Executive agency must develop a federal information systems security awareness and training plan and provide role-specific security training to employees as required by 5 CFR 930.301. The regulations advise agencies to follow the guidance published by the National Institute of Standards and Technology (NIST).

NIST publications include Special Publication 800-50, "Building an Information Technology Security Awareness and Training Program," which provides a blueprint for developing agency-specific security awareness and training materials. NIST advises agencies that users of information systems must:

☐ Understand and comply with agency security policies and procedures

☐ Be appropriately trained in the rules of behavior for their systems and applications

☐ Work with management to meet training needs

☐ Keep software/applications updated with security patches

☐ Be aware how they can better protect their agency's information; actions include, but are not limited to, proper password usage, data backup, proper antivirus protection, reporting any suspected incidents or violations of security policy, and following rules to avoid social engineering attacks and deter the spread of spam, viruses and worms

Special Publication 800-50 recommends addressing these topics in agency security awareness campaigns. Other topics may include accessing unknown email and attachments, dealing with spam, protecting against "shoulder surfing" (i.e., someone reading a document or a computer screen from behind the user), physical protection of data (e.g., from water, fire, dust or dirt, physical access), inventory and property transfer, personal use of systems at work and home, use of encryption, transmission of sensitive/confidential information, laptop security, and personally owned systems and software.

In Special Publication 800-46, "Security for Telecommuting and Broadband Communications," NIST helps federal agencies address security issues by providing recommendations on securing a variety of applications, protocols, and networking architectures to be used by teleworkers. NIST recommendations encompass the following five security principles:

1. All home networks connected to the Internet via a broadband connection should have some firewall device installed.

2. Web browsers should be configured to limit vulnerability to intrusion.

3. Operating system configuration options should be selected to increase security.

4. Selection of wireless and other home networking technologies should be in accordance with security goals.

5. Federal agencies should provide teleworking users with guidance on selecting appropriate technologies, software, and tools consistent with the agency network and security policies.

Complete texts of these and other NIST publications are available at http://csrc.nist.gov/publications/nistpubs/.

Manager Security Responsibilities

☐ Thoroughly review all telework agreements to ensure they are in compliance with agency information security policies.

☐ Ensure employees receive agency information systems security training.

☐ Work with employees to ensure they fully understand and have the technical expertise to comply with agency requirements.

☐ Invest in technology and equipment that can support success.

☐ Work with employees to develop secure systems for potentially sensitive documents and other materials.

☐ Track removal and return of potentially sensitive materials, such as personnel records.

☐ Enforce personal privacy requirements for records.

Teleworker Security Responsibilities

☐ Participate in agency information systems security training.

☐ Achieve sufficient technical proficiency to implement the required measures.

☐ Provide a high level of security to any personal or private information accessed at the telework site or transported between locations.

☐ Remain sensitive to individual rights to personal privacy.

☐ Comply with agency policies and with any additional requirements spelled out in the telework agreement.

Insurance, Taxes, and Retirement

Remember Insurance and taxes are complex and often confusing, even with "regular" full-time office workers. When dealing with telecommuters, they take even more of a "toll." They are muddied by such questions as: Who is liable if a visitor to your worker's home office slips on the front porch and breaks his arm? What kind of insurance will teleworkers need and can your company supply it? Can you help them take advantage of the pension plan available to full-time office workers?

And if that's not enough to think about, there's workers' comp. Whether or not the teleworker even receives it depends upon whether she's a W-2 (regular employee) or independent contractor. If it's the latter, the burden of proof is on you the employer to ensure that her job is outside of the court's definition of a "basic employee." If she actually is an independent contractor not covered by workers' comp, she can still sue your company for damages if she proves negligence.

And then there are taxes. Employees — especially former office workers who have may have little or no knowledge of such things -- need to be educated as to the finer points of home office deductions and keeping track of receipts, mileage, and related expenses. Their days of zipping through the simplified 1040EZ tax form may be gone forever. If your employees work in different states, you are faced with figuring out who pays what, and to whom. Good luck with that!

Unfortunately, at time of writing, much legislation, both at the federal and state (and even at the local) level is either pending or nonexistent. Until such time as laws, such as the Telecommuter Tax Act and the Georgia telework tax initiative, become a permanent part of the national/local firmament, managers are pretty much left hanging.

As manager, you are primarily responsible for the safety, benefits, and well-being of your workers. So it behooves you to become acquainted with the various options mentioned in this chapter and explore them more thoroughly as fits your particular situation. A good resource would be your company's legal department or federal or state informational Websites.

Property Insurance: Who Is Liable?

As the advertisement for the large insurance company says, "Life comes at you fast." So, who's responsible if your worker trips over their cat and falls down the stairs while brainstorming a new project or if their laptop is stolen from their home or briefcase while traveling? If you're pointing at yourself, you're going in the right direction; most established teleworking organizations operate on the premise that the home office is equivalent to the main office — at least for insurance purposes -- and it's a lot simpler to pay the premiums and

deductibles than to have the employee deal with them and then worry about reimbursing you. Employers need to handle compensation themselves and provide replacement equipment when necessary.

However, workers should also consider their personal insurance needs. Most homeowner's policies provide a minimum of coverage, and usually only for the business equipment in the residence itself. However if the loss or accident pertains to your business, they should only file one claim – with your insurance company – and the procedure for doing this needs to be set forth in the telecommuting agreement and during the underwriting process.

But what if a client comes to your worker's home office and sprains his ankle on her child's skateboard? Or if all the computers in the home (including those for personal and family use) contract a virus, wiping out the data on all the hard drives? In these cases, the employee should exempt your company from injuries claimed by third parties and other damages unrelated to the business and should be required to have insurance for these types of claims.

There's no way to cover all contingencies of course, but as far as possible, who is responsible for what liabilities should be spelled out in the telecommuting contract. Also, you might want to educate employees about various options regarding insurance, which may or may not be viable, depending upon what the job requires. For example, there are specific auto/truck add-ons for those using their vehicles for business; business interruption, which takes care of salary, utilities, etc., in case of natural and human-induced disasters; and an umbrella policy which can help with big-bucks claims, as long as initial expenses are taken care of under basic insurance. These "extras" can jack up premiums.

However, there are some basic options that can provide added coverage for the self-employed at a reasonable cost. Added onto a homeowner policy, an incidental business option rider covers most home office disasters. The in-home business policy is more specific to the kind of undertaking and its needs, and covers loss of papers and records, accounts receivable, and liabilities due to bodily injury or property damage on the part of the property/business owner. The third and most comprehensive policy only applies to independent contractors. Known as business owner's property, it generally pertains to multiple sites or production facilities outside the workplace.

Workers' Compensation

By and large, if they are considered "regular" W-2 workers (as opposed to independent contractors), telecommuters are covered under the same Workers' Comp (WC) regulations as

office employees in most states. The main point is that they are working out of their homes under the direction and for the benefit of their employers.

Most common WC-covered injuries, such as slips, trips, falls, lacerations and so forth, "tend to be few and far between on the telecommuting front," according to William Adkinson in Risk & Insurance magazine. Since they are working at home, which for most is a safe and comfortable environment, perhaps the chances of these kinds of accidents are less. Adkinson also speculates that telecommuters may be more reluctant to report incidents, since they are motivated to get the work done and are not looking for an escape hatch from the cubicle farm.

However, this is where the issue of where defining workers as regular (W-2) employees or independent contractors (IC) once again raises its head. If the worker is an independent contractor, then he or she may not be entitled to workers' compensation. However, the burden is on the employer to make sure he is truly an IC. In many instances, courts strictly apply the 20 IRS guidelines (see sidebar) to determine whether the worker in fact does fit the definition of a W-2 employee. You can check with your state's Workers' Comp office for specific regulations and guidance.

Even if the person is an IC, your company still may be liable for injuries suffered on the job. W-2 or regular employees covered by WC insurance, "in exchange for the benefits they receive for their injuries … give up the right to sue their employer for damages," points out Forbes.com. However, "ICs are not covered by workers' compensation, which means that they can sue you for damages if they are injured on the job …"

Remember Either way, it is the responsibility of the employer to ensure an environment that's as safe and risk-free as possible, whether it is at the home, the office, or even the employee's car if it's used for business.

Worker Classifications and Taxes

Before hiring, you should know whether the teleworker will be an independent contractor (IC) or regular (W-2) employee. This can be an especially slippery slope; due to the very nature of the telework arrangement, the distinction more easily becomes blurred. According to the IRS, with an independent contractor, "you, the payer, have the right to control or direct only the result of the work done … and not the means and methods of accomplishing the result." Examples of ICs would include an electrician, a transcriptionist, or anyone who works independently for several different companies or clients from a separate site (such as a home office) and who supplies their own equipment.

In contrast, an employee is anyone who performs services for you in which you control how and when it will be done. For telecommuters, this can be people who work at a call center (whether based in their homes or at a separate site) or do the majority of their work for one company, even if they are based at home. Many of these workers have full corporate jobs with benefits and are on a schedule dictated by the employer. Other employees act as underwriters, software engineers, financial analysts, and marketing managers or have jobs that can be easily measured.

Then there are statutory employees who, while they may be based at home or are otherwise away from the office, are to be treated as employees by law. Three categories particularly relevant to telecommuters include:

A full-time life insurance sales agent whose principal business activity is selling life insurance or annuity contracts, or both, primarily for one life insurance company.

An individual who works at home on materials or goods that you supply and that must be returned to you or to a person you name, if you also furnish specifications for the work to be done.

A full-time traveling or city salesperson, working on your behalf, who turns in orders to you from wholesalers, retailers, contractors, or operators of hotels, restaurants, or other similar establishments. The goods sold must be merchandise for resale or supplies for use in the buyer's business operation. The work performed for you must be the salesperson's principal business activity.

Source: IRS

Categories of Control

The relationship between the worker and the business must be examined with regards to aspects of control and independence, which have been conveniently divided into three categories by the IRS.

1. **Behavioral control:** This includes the kind of instructions given to the worker, as well as when and where they work, along with training. "The key consideration is whether the business has retained the right to control the details of a worker's performance or instead has given up that right," the IRS guidelines state. If the latter is the case, then the employee is an IC.

2. **Financial control:** This encompasses such issues as unreimbursed business expenses (usually the case with ICs, although there are exceptions); the extent of the worker's investment (ICs often invest in their own equipment and facilities); and

whether or not the individual makes their services available to the marketplace in general and/or advertise (as ICs often do). Payment is another aspect: "An employee is generally guaranteed a regular wage amount for an hourly, weekly, or other period of time ... even when the wage or salary is supplemented by a commission," the IRS guideline states. "An independent contractor is usually paid ... a flat fee for the job" although there may be exceptions.

3. **Type of relationship:** The nature of the work arrangement may be evidenced by such things as a written contract which describes the relationship; whether the business will provide employee benefits, such as a pension plan, vacation, or health insurance; and the permanency of the relationship. With the latter, employees are generally hired indefinitely, while ICs are engaged for a specific projects or time periods. Finally, the extent to which the services are a key part of the company's regular business is another aspect – if the worker's duties are so integral to the business that you must direct and control his activities then it is likely an employee-employer relationship.

The price for misclassification can be steep. If you incorrectly categorize an employee as an independent contractor, you can be held liable for benefits, as well as employment taxes, for that worker, plus a penalty. Rules change and new interpretations are common – as are misinterpretations, especially if you are unfamiliar with the nuances of the various regulations. So, it's best to consult an accountant or a labor relations expert when making this determination.

Along with other state and federal agencies, the IRS serves as a watchdog regarding this matter and has set forth guidelines and factors regarding who controls what (see sidebar). According to the IRS, you must withhold income taxes, withhold and pay Social Security and Medicare taxes, and pay unemployment tax on wages paid to an employee (Form W-2 worker). You do not generally have to withhold or pay any taxes on payments to independent contractors (Form 1099 worker).

IRS 20 Factor Test on Employment Status

1. Instructions: A worker who must comply with other persons' instructions about when, where and how he or she is to work is ordinarily an employee. This factor is present when the person for whom the services are performed has the right to require compliance.

2. Training: Requiring an experienced employee to work with the worker, corresponding with the worker, requiring the worker to attend meetings or using other training methods indicates the person for whom the services are performed wants them done in a particular method or manner.

3. Integration: Integrating the worker's services into the business operations generally shows that he or she is subject to direction and control. When the success or continuation of a business depends to an

appreciable degree on the performance of certain services, the workers who do them must necessarily be subject to a certain amount of control by the business owner.

4. Services rendered personally: If the worker must render the services personally, presumably the person for whom they are performed is interested in the methods used to accomplish the work, as well as in the results.

5. Hiring, supervising and paying assistants. If the person for whom the services are performed hires, supervises and pays assistants, that generally shows control over the workers on the job. However, if one worker hires, supervises and pays the other assistants under a contract in which the worker agrees to provide materials and labor and is responsible only for attaining a result, this indicates independent contractor status.

6. Continuing relationship: A continuing relationship between the worker and the person for whom the services are performed indicates an employer-employee relationship exists. This may occur when work is performed at frequently recurring although irregular intervals.

7. Set hours of work: If the person for whom the services are performed establishes set work hours, this indicates control.

8. Full-time required: If the worker must devote himself or herself substantially full-time to the business of the person for whom the services are performed, the latter has control over the amount of time the worker spends working and implicitly restricts the worker from doing other gainful work. An independent contractor, on the other hand, is free to work when and for whom he or she chooses.

9. Doing work on employer's premises: If the individual performs the work on the premises of the person for whom the services are performed, this suggests control over the worker, especially if the work could be done elsewhere. Work done off the premises, such as at the worker's office, indicates some freedom from control. However, this fact by itself does not mean the worker is not an employee. The importance of this factor depends on the nature of the service involved and the extent to which an employer generally would require that employees perform such services on the premises. Control over the place of work is indicated when the person for whom the services are performed has the right to compel the worker to travel a designated route, to canvass a territory within a certain time frame or work at specific places.

10. Order or sequence set: If a worker must perform services in the order or sequence set by the person for whom the services are performed, that factor shows the worker is not free to follow his or her own pattern of work but must follow the established routines and schedules of the employer. Often, because of the nature of an occupation, the person or persons for whom the services are performed do not set the order of the services or set it infrequently. Retaining the right to do so is sufficient to show control.

11. Oral or written reports: A requirement that the worker submit regular or written reports to the person or persons for whom the services are performed indicates a certain degree of control.

12. Payment by hour, week or month: Payment by one of these three methods generally points to an employer-employee relationship, provided this method is not just a convenient way of paying a lump sum agreed upon as the cost of a job. Payment made by the job or on a straight commission basis generally indicates the worker is an independent contractor.

13. **Payment of business or travel expenses:** If the person for whom the services are performed generally pays the worker's business and travel expenses, he or she is ordinarily an employee. To control expenses, an employer usually retains the right to regulate and direct the worker's business activities.

14. **Tools and materials:** The fact the person for whom the services are performed furnishes significant tools, materials and other equipment tends to show the existence of an employer-employee relationship.

15. **Significant investment:** If the worker invests in facilities not typically maintained by employees, such as an office rented at fair value from an unrelated party, and uses them to perform services, that tends to indicate the worker is an independent contractor. On the other hand, lack of investment in facilities indicates dependence on the person for whom the services are performed for such facilities. Accordingly, an employer-employee relationship exists.

16. **Realization of profit or loss:** A worker who can realize a profit or suffer a loss as a result of his or her services (in addition to the profit or loss ordinarily realized by employees) is generally an independent contractor. The worker who cannot is an employee. For example, if a worker is subject to a real risk of economic loss due to a significant investment or a bona fide liability for expenses, such as salary payments to unrelated employees, that indicates the worker is an independent contractor. The risk a worker will not receive payment for his or her services, however, is common to both independent contractors and employees and thus is not sufficient to support independent contractor treatment.

17. **Working for more than one entity:** If a worker performs more than de minimis services for multiple unrelated persons or companies at the same time, that factor generally indicates the worker is an independent contractor. However, a worker who performs services for more than one person may be an employee of each, especially where the two are connected.

18. **Making service available to the general public:** The fact a worker makes his or her services available to the general public on a regular and consistent basis indicates an independent contractor relationship.

19. **Right to discharge:** The right to fire a worker is a factor indicating the worker is an employee and the person with the right is an employer. An employer exercises control through the threat of dismissal, which causes the worker to obey the employer's instructions. An independent contractor, on the other hand, cannot be fired so long as he or she produces a result that meets the agreed contract specifications.

20. **Right to terminate:** If the worker has the right to end his or her relationship with the person for whom the services are performed at any time without incurring liability, this indicates an employer-employee relationship.

Source: IRS

Teleworker Tax Responsibilities

For the workers themselves, and this applies whether they are full-time W-2s or independent contractors, along with keeping records on monies received and reimbursed expenses (backed up with check stubs and receipts), they should keep and maintain records of all expenditures, even if it means throwing them in a box and handing them over to an accountant on April 14. Needless to say, the cost of doing that might offset any potential refund! These should be turned in along with W-2 forms and for ICs, 1099s, of which

there may be several if they are working for different companies. You, as an employer, are responsible for making sure they receive 1099s if they earn over $600 a year.

Another issue facing workers is whether their home office even qualifies for a deduction. If the primary place where they conduct business is the company office, or a telework center, then they may not meet the criteria. According to the Website, www.powerbizhome.com, the business part of the home must be the principal place where workers meet or deal with patients, clients or customers or, if it's a trade or business, a separate structure that's not attached to the home. However, even if the worker's home office does not qualify, she can still deduct all legitimate business expenses. Employees can be directed to Websites (such as www.irs.gov/newsroom/article/0,,id=108138,00.html) and written information (often found in the public library) from the IRS as to what is and what is not deductible.

If that's as clear as mud, the tax issues facing companies are even more confusing. Not surprisingly, most of the mess arises from intrastate (and by extension intra-county and -city) taxes. Telecommuters often work in one state and live in another, where they also work part of the time. Obviously, this has huge and conflicting consequences in terms of state unemployment insurance and state income taxes. Some organizations process payroll for each state where the teleworker is located.

Retirement Alternatives

Some companies offer pension plans to telecommuters, most do not. The equitable rule – the same benefits apply whether they're working at home or in office – regarding pension plans tends to be less stringent regarding telecommuters. While telecommuters may have leverage when it comes to full-coverage health insurance and workers' comp, they are pretty much on their own for pension plans. However, you can provide some basic information about the various retirement fund alternatives and, if possible, make arrangements for your telecommuters to participate in the company plan.

The following is an overview of the most common pension plans:

☐ **401(k) Plan** – Here the employee defers part of his current income – the limit changes each year – into a tax shelter where it grows tax-free until he withdraws it. In some cases, the employer matches the employee's contributions. The beauty of this plan is that it allows an employee to save for retirement and simultaneously reduce her current income tax bill. Employees can also make decisions as to the investment of these funds.

☐ **Defined Benefit Pension Plan** – This traditional pension plan pays workers a specific monthly benefit at retirement, either by stating it as an exact dollar amount or a specific formula that calculates the benefit. Generally, the company funds the pension plan, and a professional money manager invests the assets of the fund.

☐ **Qualified Retirement Plan** – A qualified retirement plan is established by a business and includes profit sharing, defined benefits, and money purchase pensions. Employees' contributions to a qualified plan are not taxed until they withdraw the money. In addition, any contributions made to the plan on the worker's behalf by the employer are tax deductible.

☐ **Individual Retirement Account (Traditional)** – A practical alternative for teleworkers, especially if they are ICs, IRAs are established by individuals, not companies. Covered by a different section of the tax code, they are not retirement plans per se. At the time of writing, under this plan, an individual can deposit up to $5,000 of earned income a year into an IRA ($6,000 if you're 50 or over). If an individual is not eligible to participate in the company's pension, profit sharing, or 401(k) plan – in essence, many teleworkers -- the contributions to the IRA are deductible irrespective of their income. However, if the individual is covered by a company retirement plan and/ or if her adjusted gross income exceeds certain levels, she loses the right to an IRA deduction. Traditional IRA earnings are taxed when they are withdrawn.

☐ **Roth Individual Retirement Account** – This is similar to the traditional IRA except the contributions to a Roth IRA are nondeductible. When you withdraw money from a Roth IRA in retirement, it will be tax-free.

☐ **Keogh Plan** – This is a qualified retirement plan for self-employed individuals, especially independent contractors or consultants who work for several companies. Contributions to this plan are tax-deductible. The individual can direct the investment of the funds that are put into a Keogh, e.g., stocks, bonds, or mutual funds.

Adapted from: Findlaw.com

Regardless of their status, all employee contributions to retirement plans are subject to protection under law.

ERISA and Teleworkers

The Employee Retirement Income Security Act of 1974, or ERISA, protects the assets of millions of Americans so that funds placed in retirement plans during their working lives will be there when they retire. ERISA is a federal law that sets minimum standards for pension plans in private industry. For example, if your company maintains a pension plan, ERISA specifies when the employees must be allowed to become a participant, how long they have

to work before they have a non-forfeitable interest in the pension, how long they can be away from their jobs before it might affect their benefits, and whether spouses have a right to part of the pension in the event of the worker's death. Most of the provisions of ERISA are effective for plan years beginning on or after January 1, 1975.

However, ERISA does not require any employer to establish a pension plan. It only requires that those who do establish plans must meet certain minimum standards. The law generally does not specify how much money a participant must be paid as a benefit.

Source: U.S. Department of Labor

Social "in"Security

Traditionally, Social Security provided "a base of economic security … through a valuable package of retirement, disability and survivors insurance," according to the U.S. Department of Labor (DOL).

The DOL estimates that about 163 million workers are paying into the Social Security system, with another approximately 50 million people currently receiving retirement, survivors and disability benefits.

Originally designed to link how much workers and their employers pay into the system over their actual years on the job and how much they will get in benefits, Social Security allowed high-wage earners to receive a higher benefit payment than low-wage earners.

However, given the potential drain caused by the pending retirement of millions of Baby Boomers and the smaller actual working population paying into the system after their departure, Social Security will be put under a severe financial strain in the coming years. Therefore, it behooves both your company and your workers to look at additional alternatives to supplement their retirement plans. With telecommuters, it may mean investigating several of the alternatives mentioned here.

Two Landmark Teleworker Cases

Zelinsky v. Tax Appeals Tribunal of New York – The Cardozo Law School of New York in New York City employed Edward Zelinsky, a Connecticut resident, as a law professor. Zelinsky worked at the law school several days a week, lecturing and meeting with students. The rest of the time, he worked in his Connecticut home, grading student assignments and conducting work-related legal research.

Connecticut regards the work done in-state to be taxable in Connecticut based on the point-of-presence test. New York, however, regards all work done by Zelinsky as taxable in

New York because Cardozo Law School could have instructed its employee to work in New York. Taxed in both states on the same income, Zelinsky took his case to court.

The New York Court of Appeals found against him [citing] the "convenience of the employer" when an employee's work location was not required by the employer for hard business reasons. The case was then appealed to the U.S. Supreme Court, which declined to review it.

Thomas Huckaby v. New York State Division of Taxation – Thomas L. Huckaby, a computer programmer, lived and worked mainly in Tennessee. His Tennessee-based employer went out of business in 1991. In 1994, Huckaby was hired by a New York-based company to support software purchased from his former employer. Huckaby, who never lived in New York, spent 75 percent of the time between 1994 and 1995 working in Tennessee and 25 percent working in New York. He reported as New York wages only those wages earned while on visits to the corporate office in New York. Since his employer could have relocated him to New York (but did not), New York claimed that Huckaby's working in Tennessee was "for the convenience of the employer," and all wages earned were subject to New York taxes.

In a four-to-three decision, the New York Court of Appeals found for the state of New York. In a dissenting opinion, Judge Robert Smith stated: "The majority cites no authority at all, and offers no persuasive reason, in support of this new interpretation."

Source: IOMA Payroll Manager's Report

However, out of lemons occasionally emerges something resembling lemonade. The adverse ruling in the Zelinsky case led to the introduction of the Telecommuter Tax Fairness Act of 2004 by Connecticut Senators Christopher Dodd and Joseph Lieberman and U.S. Representative Christopher Shay. No action was taken on the bill in 2004; it was reintroduced in May of 2005 and then again in May 2007 by Shay. As of the time of writing it has still not passed.

And thanks, no doubt in part, to the controversy generated by the Huckaby case, New York issued a memorandum that said, effective retroactively to January 1, 2006, for nonresidents with a primary office in New York and a bona fide employer office at home, income for any day worked at home will not be subject to New York state income tax. Gee, thanks!

A 2006 law passed in Georgia rewards employers who implement teleworking programs by giving them a tax credit of up to $1,200 per employee for a percentage of their telework expenses in calendar years 2008 and 2009. The program's success will be evaluated by the Department of Revenue in 2010.

Health Care Options

Given the current healthcare crisis in the U.S., offering full or even partial coverage for health insurance premiums can be a major carrot for potential employees. You have only to look at the retirees employed by Wal-Mart or those with PhDs and Masters' degrees who work at Starbucks. Although they may be making close to minimum wage, that's not the point. They are no longer among the ranks of the 47 million Americans (16 percent of the population) who are without coverage. As of the time of writing, President Obama's healthcare reform plan had just been enacted into law. Although some provisions of The Patient Protection and Affordable Healthcare Act are to be effective by the fall of 2010, much of the legislation is not fully operational until 2014.

However, health insurance costs have become so exorbitant that even full-time employees are paying partial or a la carte coverage for certain services, such as dental or vision. So depending upon your company's policy towards W-2 and part-time workers, you may not have much of a choice. The bottom line is that teleworkers should be treated the same as office workers if they have the same duties. For example, if health insurance is provided to part-timers in the office, the same should apply to those who work at home or on the road.

You can also assist employees in getting the best deal possible. Oftentimes companies employ consultants or in-house specialists whose job it is to provide the most comprehensive and cost-effective health coverage for their workers. Sharing this information with employees is helpful, as is suggesting that they check out a group plan from their trade or professional association or even a local chamber of commerce. Many associations of independent contractors – such as writer's organizations, for example – offer reduced-cost health coverage to qualifying members.

Becoming increasingly popular is the Health Savings Account (HSA) – also known as a medical savings account (MSA) – which allows workers to allot pretax dollars to cover out-of-pocket expenses. Employees can set aside as much as $2,900 for singles and $5,800 for families in these accounts, which can be used to reimburse medical, dental and vision expenses not covered by health insurance. These figures are for 2008 and generally go up every year to cover cost-of-living increases. Employers can also make HSA contributions for workers which are also excluded from income and not subject to any income tax or FICA. Most states also allow state income tax deductions for HSA contributions.

Accompanied by a High Deductible Health Plan (HDHP), HSA funds are not subject to federal income tax at the time of deposit. They can be used to pay for qualified medical expenses at any time without federal tax liability. However, should you decide to make a

withdrawal for non-medical expenses, depending on your age you would be subject to the same penalties as if it were an IRA account. The savings accounts can be used to help pay smaller covered medical expenses until the deductible is met; the high deductible insurance policy then takes care of covered medical expenses exceeding the deductible.

HSAs are useful because they help keep down health care costs while providing an opportunity to accrue a tax-free financial nest egg in the event of an illness. A health savings plan also allows you to choose your own physician (typically from an extensive PPO directory) without the restrictions imposed by HMO-type plans. However, it may not be viable or practical if the worker has pre-existing conditions or healthcare coverage from another source.

STEP FIVE: MAINTENANCE – ENSURING A SMOOTH FLOW OF OPERATIONS

The Importance of Trust

Remember

Trust is especially important in telecommuting, because there is so much physical distance between you and your workers. This is true of every job, from call center employees to high-level executives who manage dozens of virtual teams around the globe. If you believe your employees are doing their job properly – and if they think you are providing competent and fair guidance and direction – then things will move along smoothly most of the time.

However, if you don't trust them for any reason, then it's time to take stock. Either you are buying into the Big Brother mentality that they are children and must be watched every minute – which doesn't make for a healthy work environment under any conditions – or certain red flags have popped up causing an undermining of trust. These include:

- ☐ Job performance starts to suffer, either in quantity or quality of results.
- ☐ Absenteeism starts to increase.
- ☐ You, or the teleworker's co-workers, start having communication problems – either decreased or poorer communication.
- ☐ The teleworker shows less interest in attending department meetings or otherwise shows signs of becoming a "loner." Don't confuse this with signs of irritation at ill-organized and rambling meetings. Teleworkers tend to become more time-conscious and agenda-oriented as they gain experience.

From Managing Telework, Jack Nilles, p.115

Before jumping to conclusions, however, your next step is to get more information from the teleworker herself. Sit down with her and have an open discussion, asking how she feels about the work and be objective about your various concerns. "The teleworker might be having problems adjusting to the new routine, or still be trying to work out the fine points of scheduling his or her time," observes author Jack Nilles. "Sometimes the relative independence [of teleworking] can be overwhelming and more detailed supervision can help." If things continue to worsen, then you may need to take disciplinary or corrective action.

Tips

An easy way of establishing trust is to work with a known quantity; that is, employees who have been with your organization for a while and/or with whom you have a rapport or workers experienced in their field who can provide references or have a proven track record. However, circumstances may be such that you may have to go "outside" and hire someone completely new. In that case, networking can come in handy; for example, a colleague or peer can recommend a worker within the organization or field of endeavor. Local colleges or trade schools can be especially helpful in supplying recent graduates or leads, especially if you are looking for teleworkers in a geographic area with which you're unfamiliar. Likewise, personnel or temp agencies can be a source of reliable clerical or customer support referrals although, of course, most charge for this service.

Many times your instincts will tell you who to trust. Does the worker appear to learn quickly and display enthusiasm during training and in your various communications? Does she express an interest in the company and its goals along with a willingness to learn new things? Does she make that extra effort to satisfy the customer or end user rather than shrugging and saying, "It's not my job?" Is she willing to participate in meetings, either onsite or remotely, to get to know members of the team and share information? During training, if a new hire seems unresponsive or disengaged, you might want to watch them closely to make sure they're actually capable (and willing) to do the job.

Most of us have an internal trip wire that goes off whenever we encounter someone who may not be trustworthy. Often this is triggered by such cues as a lack of eye contact or a bored tone of voice or just a sense that their personality might not mesh well with the team. Because you are not physically seeing the individual or probably even speaking with him daily, telecommuting adds an extra layer of distance, so it's especially important to have a positive "gut feeling" about this person, whether you're meeting him face-to-face or over the phone. When it comes to establishing trust, there's no substitute for either type of contact during the interview process.

Once the person is hired, you can take specific steps to foster trust among team members.

Open and honest communication: The only way employees will know what you're thinking is if you tell them directly.

Give trust to get trust: This can seem like a bit of a risk, especially if you've been accustomed to managing workers in an office. But "leading by example" sets the stage for an atmosphere of mutual trust and encourages others to trust you back. Remember, "Innocent until proven guilty?" Especially at the beginning, if you communicate mistrust, then it may very well condemn the team – and the project -- to an atmosphere of negativity and suspicion.

Honesty is always the best policy: Although they are physically removed from the rumor mill and corporate politics, telecommuters still hear things. However, if you are upfront with them about the good, bad, and the not-so-certain, they will feel they can come to you with questions and concerns. If you are bound by confidentiality in not revealing specific information – say, a corporate takeover and/or layoffs are imminent but nothing is confirmed – then tell them you do not yet have concrete answers (the truth), and you will get back with them as soon as you know something for sure.

Even if you make a mistake or don't know something, it's better to admit that than try to cover it up or "bs" your way out of it. Most people can sense when they are being stonewalled and nothing undermines trust faster than that.

Establish a core set of business ethics: These basic standards of honesty, decency, and behavior should be set forth as part of the company culture and work plan and agreed upon, understood, and internalized by all team members. Ethics are the glue which hold teams together, and are especially important to those separated by time and space, allowing them operate under common beliefs and the same principles.

Follow through: If you say you're going to do something, do it, and do it out loud. Team members should know that for better or worse, if you say it, you'll "git 'r' done." Don't be like the joke, "Do what I say, not what I do."

Be consistent: This works well both in sports and in business. If your team members know you're going to react logically and fairly to mistakes and problems, then they will be more willing to approach you. Unpredictable reactions, however, elicit the opposite response and can set the stage for cover-ups and misunderstandings.

Be responsive and available: This can be tricky, given variances in time zones and work hours. No matter how you implement the system of communication, employees need to know you'll get back to them within a certain time.

Ask questions: Diverse teams may use different cultural slang and points of reference. Be sensitive to these, and ask for clarification to avoid confusion and misunderstandings. This is true whether you're dealing with face-to-face meetings, teleconferences, or written communications, such as emails.

Be trustworthy: Sometimes employees will come to you with personal information or express concerns about work-related matters or even personality conflicts. As with office workers, it's important to keep this confidential, even if they are scattered around the globe. The best way to keep a secret is to keep it to yourself.

Be generous with praise and include everyone: Professional development classes, incentives, and social gatherings, even if they are infrequent and informal, help build and cement relationships. Take the time to get to know your team members, and ask about their families and hobbies (making sure not to get too personal of course, or break any confidences). For example, workers "bond" during ARO virtual training seminars by sharing their hobbies and interests with the group.

Performance Evaluation

Remember Managing performance is a fairly simple process: define the job, communicate requirements, monitor that requirements are being met, and recognize and reward progress. These basic elements should have little if anything to do with whether the employee is an office worker or a teleworker.

Job definitions have the same components and the measurements should apply to component tasks. The only variation would be where the components of the job can best be performed – at the office, at the telework center or other offsite location, or at home. Discussing this could help the teleworker plan his or her days, both at and away from the office.

When it comes to communicating job requirements, the job description should be the same for both teleworkers and other staff. However, if the teleworking employee is new and unfamiliar with the organization, you might want to provide more detailed process guides than for office workers whom you'd be seeing on a day-to-day basis. Discussions and briefings can be scheduled for when the teleworker is in the office and the telephone and email can easily substitute when necessary.

Action plans and 'to do' lists can be a useful communication tool when managing teleworkers. They provide an ongoing reminder of priority tasks and help maintain focus and productivity. They can also be an important way of monitoring performance and provide an agenda for any conversations with managers and colleagues when they are back in the office.

Key performance indicators and project milestones should be the same for teleworkers as office workers.

Meeting and discussing team performance and its contribution to the organization's goals is important for the teleworker, more so than for onsite staff as it keeps teleworkers in touch with what is happening around the organization. As with office workers, each teleworker's performance should be discussed on a regular basis.

The answer to the question "How do I manage staff I can't see?" is usually another question: "How do you manage staff now?" If you already manage on a resourcing-and-measuring-outcomes basis, very little will change when an employee becomes a teleworker.

Disciplinary Issues

Consistency and fairness are bywords when it comes to managing all workers, whether in or outside of the office. However, despite your best intentions and careful planning, sometimes problems arise. The teleworker may decide to bail because she misses the camaraderie of the office, or you may find that productivity or customer service is suffering.

Tips

Whatever the cause, act immediately rather than wait. Deal directly with problems, rather than avoiding them. However, make sure the method of communication you use fits the situation.

For example, if the issue is minor – the employee fails to turn in a report, or makes a small error in documentation – a simple email in the form of a "gentle reminder" will suffice. However, if the infraction is more serious and persistent – being rude to customers or failing to follow up on an important lead – then further action may be necessary, such as a face-to-face meeting, or a one-on-one video or telephone conference. Under no circumstances should managers hide behind technology to circumvent confrontation, such as firing someone by email (when no previous discipline was attempted) or texting them that they screwed up. The same standards should apply to all workers whether in or outside of the office; and most realize that a steady job – especially one from home -- is desirable in an economy where unemployment is rampant.

To avoid creating an adversarial atmosphere, keep the conversation to "just the facts" -- the "who, what, when, and where" of the problem – and then ask to hear the employee's side of the story.

During such a discussion, managers should do the following:

☐ Have notes and make use of them. Sometimes it may be more difficult to document occurrences, but keep records as detailed as possible.

☐ Explain facts thoroughly and objectively.

☐ Pay close attention to the employee's perspective and reactions.

☐ Expect and allow emotional venting.

☐ Be specific about consequences if problems continue.

☐ Provide a system for follow-up that is both solution and results-oriented.

Adapted from: Telecommuting: Managing Offsite Staff for Small Business

Generally, discipline should be handled in a progressive manner, that is: when the problem first starts manifesting itself, it's time for an informal chat, as soon as (or immediately after) the incident occurs. Often that does the trick, but if repeated reminders fail to have any effect, then you must move onto the next level. Some misconduct may be governed by more stringent disciplinary action as dictated by company policy. The manager is responsible for knowing their company's procedures for investigation and disciplinary action.

Tips

Whenever possible, put a positive spin on discipline, couching it as a "call to improvement" rather than a punitive action. Also always make sure to follow company policy to the letter regarding discipline. As a manager, you're responsible for making sure all your actions are fully and correctly documented.

Teleworker Termination – Maybe not "The End"

Remember

Unlike office employees, telecommuters are held to different standards of discipline. Because the arrangement is voluntary in nearly all cases, and considered a privilege for the employee, the progression of action – reprimands, probation, demotion/reassignment, and suspension – may not be followed as closely.

Rather, solutions are more immediate and may include:

☐ Rescinding the telework arrangement

☐ Modifying the telework agreement to better define your expectations

☐ Setting a time frame for the employee to demonstrate a significant improvement

☐ Resolving other circumstances that may have contributed to the unsatisfactory performance

Source: Office of Personnel Management

Often telecommuting problems deal with circumstances surrounding the home work arrangement, such as toddler tension or eldercare. Or the worker may need additional training or is having equipment difficulties. Sometimes these issues can be resolved; on other occasions, not. Regardless, you need to document times, dates, and any other information that may lead up to your decision, being very specific about what transpired, what was discussed, and when the various conversations/problems occurred.

The worker needs to know about each infraction, and understand what will happen if she fails to improve. This information should be documented and signed off on by all parties.

The end of the telecommuting arrangement doesn't necessarily mean the worker needs to leave the company. If she is productive and valuable, she may be better suited to the office, particularly if she'd succeeded there before telecommuting. However, whether she's working from her basement or a cubicle in the middle of headquarters, she needs to be held to the same standards of performance. This should be made clear regardless of the final outcome or decision.

The Final Solution?

In the bricks and mortar world, employee termination usually takes place face-to-face. Few things are more indicative of weak management than hiding behind emails, faxes, or other technology to avoid the unpleasantness of letting someone go. However, in the universe of telecommuting, workers can be far-flung and removed from their managers. So, there may be no choice other than to fire over the phone. Regardless of how it's done, termination needs to be accomplished in a fair, equitable, and calm manner.

Circumstances for firing may vary: it could be because every avenue has been tried and exhausted to improve performance/behavior; the job itself has evolved and the person is unable to adapt; or that the worker has committed an act or misconduct – such as sexual harassment or drug use – and the only choice is to let him go.

Regardless of how or when you fire, make sure that the time and place is private. Only those who are directly involved -- managerial personnel, witnesses -- should be told in advance and, if necessary, present. Having a third party in the room is usually a good idea, "someone who understands the gravity of the situation and who will hold the discussion and details of the termination to be confidential in nature," according to management expert Malcolm Tatum.

Also, be very specific in discussing the circumstances of the firing, citing names, dates, and statistics related to the job and other information, such as final pay, expense reports, health insurance, and so on. If severance is being offered or unemployment is available, include details on that, as well.

With home-based workers, there is less security and, thus, greater concerns about breaches of confidentiality or dissemination of private information. However, such contingencies should have been covered in the initial telecommuter agreement. If circumstances dictate, you might want to gently remind the employee that he signed a confidentiality/security agreement, and it is legally binding.

Tips

Terminations are emotional, and the team member may not hear what you've said the first time, so you may have to repeat yourself to make sure he's understood everything. Also give him the information in writing, and depending upon the circumstances, perhaps some words of encouragement about finding a better situation with another company that's more commensurate with his skills and needs.

Performance Appraisals

Office managers have the advantage of sitting down with employees face-to-face and evaluating their performance. This gives them the benefit of softening criticism with cues, such as an apologetic smile or an encouraging tap on the arm. Such body language goes a long way in helping the worker internalize and understand what you are trying to communicate. Plus, facing someone directly through one-on-one conversation facilitates a deeper and more comfortable discussion. Even the act of handing someone a Kleenex invites confidences.

Distance managers have no such luxury. Often when you evaluate performance, it's over the phone or via email, two mediums which, by their very limitations, can facilitate misunderstanding, hurt feelings and resentment. So how do you overcome these obstacles, resulting in a positive and objective learning experience for both you and the employee?

Defining key measures and areas of responsibility are also essential in evaluating performance. Thus, each team member is aware of his "arena of power" and how well he/she is performing at any given time.

Evaluating Program Success

Worker Satisfaction

Your telework program will grow and change with your organization. Evaluating your program is the best way for your company to know what and how to improve and might include the following questions for teleworkers:

1. Is your telework schedule flexible enough?
2. Have your relationships changed?
3. Has your job changed?
4. Identify any resources that you use regularly and are usually available in the office, but are difficult to access when you are teleworking, such as reference books or archival files.
5. Identify any equipment needs that you could use at home to improve your effectiveness and productivity.

6. What has worked well/increased your effectiveness?

7. What has caused problems/made you less effective?

8. How has teleworking changed the way you do your job to facilitate teleworking?

9. What skills have you strengthened due to teleworking?

10. How do you feel that teleworking enhances or undermines the organization's overall goals and culture?

11. If you were to give advice to a co-worker who was about to start teleworking, what would it be?

The only way to know if your employees are really satisfied is to ask. Many of the following questions are open-ended; there is no "right" answer.

☐ How has telecommuting contributed to your personal goals?

☐ Are you more or less satisfied with work now that you're telecommuting?

☐ How has telecommuting affected your home life and family relationships?

☐ Has it increased or decreased your job stress?

☐ Do you feel you're working longer/harder than your office counterparts?

☐ Do you feel isolated from your coworkers?

☐ Do you feel they resent your telecommuting arrangement?

☐ How do you feel telecommuting has affected your relationship with your manager?

☐ Do you feel being a telecommuter will hold you back in your career? Why or why not?

☐ What are your work habits? Do you have trouble concentrating? Or are you working nonstop?

☐ Overall, do you think telecommuting has been a success for you personally? Why or why not?

Adapted from: An Organizational Guide to Telecommuting

Getting and soliciting regular feedback will not only help solidify and improve work operations, but will also boost morale, increase and improve communication, facilitate trust and strengthen relationships.

Tips

Manager Satisfaction

In order for the program to work efficiently and effectively, managers need to be satisfied, as well. It may take time to adjust and overcome initial resistance to a new way of working, as discussed earlier. But once you've been managing telecommuters for a while, take some time to evaluate whether you think the telecommuting program is working, and why. Are workers

meeting their goals and mileposts? Are communications smooth and responses to problems quick and easily resolved? If other office workers are a part of the team, what are their attitudes towards teleworkers and how does this affect your role as a manager? Additionally:

☐ When conducting performance evaluations, do you find that you assess a teleworker's performance differently from an office worker's?

☐ Can you easily and comfortably evaluate employee performance?

☐ Is there a sense of camaraderie and teamwork in the department?

☐ Do you communicate with telework employees any differently when they are working away from the office?

☐ Are telecommuters more difficult to manage than office workers? If so, in what way?

☐ Does managing telecommuters involve extra work? How much and why?

☐ Are performance problems more difficult to handle? Do you have more or fewer performance problems with teleworkers?

☐ How has the productivity of your employees changed since they began teleworking?

☐ Has your management style changed since you or your employees began teleworking?

☐ Does teleworking create more work for you?

Answering these and any other questions related to communication, productivity, and employee attitudes (yours and team members') will help provide insight into the success of the overall effort.

Customer Satisfaction

This can be a difficult and evasive area to evaluate. For one thing, many organizations and companies don't necessarily want their customers to know they're utilizing telecommuters. It should make no difference whether the person answering the customer service inquiry or investigating the insurance claim is working from a wheelchair, or a thousand miles away in Hawaii. However, there are indirect ways of finding out whether the telecommuting effort is benefiting your customers.

The big picture: Is your customer base growing? Are you getting plenty of positive feedback or more complaints? Do things seem to be running more (or less) smoothly since you've instituted telecommuters?

Surveys: These can be done over the telephone, the Internet via an interactive Website or by sending emails, or the old-fashioned paper-consuming snail mail way. Questions can revolve around the quality and ease of interactions and communications, as well as the responsiveness

of the individual and resolution of the problem and/or question. A rating scale ("From 1-10") can be used or they can check yes or no answers. Surveys should be short and sometimes have an incentive attached, such as a coupon or discount to encourage customers to respond.

Focus groups: Here a group is asked about their attitude toward a product, service, idea or packaging. Focus groups are effective in evaluating services or testing new ideas. Because they generally involve a smaller number of people and/or take a longer amount of time (from a couple of hours to even several days), you can get in-depth information and insights not normally obtained from the other customer service inquiry methods. However, if numbers are what you're looking for, you may not get the scope of response that you may need.

Measuring customer satisfaction can be subjective, so it should be evaluated in conjunction with other factors, such as profit and loss, productivity, and so forth.

Tips

Rewarding Teleworkers

Celebrating the accomplishments of your workers and honoring them is just as important, and a lot more pleasant. Although telecommuting can be a reward in itself, it's not enough; even the most far-flung virtual worker in Antarctica wants to celebrate with his team when a project is successfully completed.

There are, of course, the more conventional rewards, such as bonuses, raises, time off, honorary awards (for example, a plaque or certificate), and informal recognitions, such as after-work cocktails "on the company." But these are based on the traditional office structure. Telecommuting has widened the playing field in terms of time, space and culture, so organizations might want to re-tool their incentives.

All workers should be included, both in the office and out, even if it's going for a celebratory pizza. If possible, bring in all employees for the event, and if they're so remote that this is impractical, provide a comparable incentive. For example, if the home office is participating in a training session, then make sure the employee is scheduled for a similar-type class in his home town. If the office gang has box seats to a sporting event or theatre to recognize the team effort, then all distant employees should receive tickets for something equitable in their locale. The point is that distance should be no barrier for providing either coaching or rewards and the telecommuter is a valuable and recognized member of the team, regardless of where she lives.

When Programs Fail

What they say about the dating prospects in Alaska – "The odds are good, but the goods are odd" – can pretty much apply to the success of many telecommuting efforts. According to a 2004 study by Gartner, a technology research and advisory company based in Stamford, Connecticut, an estimated 20 percent of employees who volunteer for telecommuting want to go back to the office within six months of working at home.

Programs can fail for a number of reasons. "Sometimes telework ceases to make sense in a particular environment," Bob Fortier, president of InnoVisions Canada, told Techrepublic. com. "Perhaps a new project requires intense onsite participation. Or there is a decline in the quality or quantity of an employee's work. Or it could be because the telework arrangement had a negative impact on others in the work unit."

Other factors contributing to failure may include:

1. Lack of quality face time where a high level of interaction is needed. As discussed in the early chapters of this book, certain types of jobs and work situations lend themselves to telecommuting; others do not.

2. The need for the worker's actual physical presence in getting the job done. Again, this depends upon the situation; if a high level of coordination and communication is required, doing it "from a distance" may be counterproductive.

3. Loss of creativity. Some jobs, such as advertising campaigns, require frequent brainstorming sessions where team members meet constantly and bounce ideas off each other.

4. Disconnect between expectations and reality. Once workers begin telecommuting, they may find it not quite the idyll (or ideal) they expected; hence the 20 percent "dropout" rate.

5. The company hired the wrong type of person without considering whether their personality and work habits suit the telework arrangement. Blanket hiring of in-house employees for telecommuting jobs can be a mistake. At the very least, the employees should be trained, evaluated, and monitored regarding their ability to handle distance work.

The First Six Months: Toughing it Out

You've worked hard to set up the telecommuting program, and believe it will be cost-effective and increase the quality of workers' lives and productivity. But it's early in the process, and employees are

coming to you with complaints about family interruptions and inability to get started and stay focused. Plus, they miss their co-workers.

What to do? Adjusting to non-office life can be difficult if you're accustomed to being around others all the time. But certain steps can ease the transition.

Tips

If they're physically nearby, allow them to come into the office for one to two days a week. This will give workers their "fix" of being around others in the office and provide valuable face-to-face time. Additionally, it may help office workers see that telecommuting is more difficult than it appears and will help forestall resentment and jealousy.

Encourage them to join a local professional association where they can meet regularly with their peers. This will keep them abreast of the latest developments and fire up creativity.

Suggest that they add a favorite sport or hobby to their weekly agenda. Again, this gets them get out of the house on a regular basis.

Provide as much support as possible. This can take the form of tech support in helping them fine-tune their computer system to meet the needs of the job to administrative assistance in sending out letters and other correspondence. Sometimes just listening to workers' concerns and letting them vent their frustrations helps, as well.

The period of adjustment generally lasts between six to 12 months, but if that has passed and things don't seem to be improving, then it's time to take stock and re-evaluate whether telecommuting is right for the department and/or jobs.

Steps for Long-Term Success

Deal With the "Mommy (or Daddy) Syndrome"

Tips

The telecommuter is hired, trained, and eager to get started in her home office. But there's a little problem – three-year-old Johnny; and Grandma, who needs to be taken to her many doctor's appointments; and the parrot which keeps chattering when the worker is on a business call. And what about the next-door neighbor who's dependent on your new teleworker to continue providing daycare/companionship for her toddler daughter while she goes to the office? Suddenly your worker's not so promising anymore – she's frazzled and pulled in many different directions and not getting the job done.

You may have tried to explain these and other challenges in advance, but until the employee is actually in the situation, she may not realize how daunting and counterproductive the many demands of home/work life can be. The following are some suggestions to help workers through the transition:

Insist that the worker have his own space, preferably a room with a door in a quiet area of the home. This can be a condition of even getting the job. Because people have to physically go there to speak with the employee, by its very nature a separate work space lends itself to fewer distractions and interruptions.

Set ground rules for interruptions. The teleworker needs to sit down with friends, neighbors, and family members and let them know the specific hours that she's "on duty" and not to be interrupted unless it's a dire emergency. This will likely mean hiring a babysitter to watch the kids/elderly parents and/or take them to daycare. When friends call or drop by, the telecommuter can gently but firmly tell them she will get back to them when she's not working.

Gain support. At first families and significant others may feel that the telecommuter's presence is a license to interrupt or ask for favors or additional help. Children may resent having to be quiet and "leave Mommy (or Daddy) alone." At the beginning of the arrangement, the telecommuter needs to explain that the condition of the job (and the paycheck) is that he needs to be solely dedicated to performing the assigned work and that he needs their help and support in this endeavor. Without it, he will be unable to telecommute.

Keep children, pets, and personal life away from professional contacts. There's nothing more off-putting than calling a number for business and hearing a young child's babble on the voicemail. Kids do pick up the phone, and most people understand this, but the message on the answering machine is within the parents' control. And as much as workers may love their dogs and/or cats, they need to make sure that barking, meowing, and other noises can't be heard over the phone, most especially if they are in customer service or call center positions.

Compartmentalize

A major difficulty faced by beginning telecommuters is the need to "separate" home from work life and sometimes even act as if they are in an office when, in fact, they are at, say, a soccer game. Although some people seem to get away with it, dividing work and home life – and kid/husband time and work time – into two compartments is the best way to ensure long-term telecommuting success. It may mean paying extra for a babysitter and at times working at a library, coffeehouse or other quiet place when the family is at home. Other teleworkers have the additional option of "hoteling" and/or working from a telework center, both discussed earlier.

Experts have found that, under certain circumstances, telecommuting can even be more stressful than office work, especially for those who have families. According to a Michigan State University study of 95 supervisors and 300 employees, home workers and those with flexible schedules actually reported more conflicts between family and work. However, those who set firm boundaries were able to handle the nontraditional work arrangement, even if it meant not picking up the phone after certain hours or staying away from the work email account on weekends. The study also found that women were less able to set limits than

men and that female managers had greater conflicts with family and work than those in less responsible jobs.

Telecommuters – especially those who are at the office part-time – can also suffer from the "two-briefcase syndrome." They must deal with maintaining two workplaces, carrying files from one office to another or even having separate briefcases for each (any security concerns will need to be dealt with beforehand). Compartmentalizing can help alleviate this – decide which records belong where, make copies for reference in both places, and plan for what you will require and when, and soon there may be no need for a briefcase at all – or only a small one. And while you're at it, suggest that workers group like tasks together; for example, making all phone calls at once, sending faxes and emails at a specific time. Along with helping them become better organized, they will be more comfortable with the telecommuting routine.

Avoid Overwork and Procrastination

Compartmentalizing also helps avoid overwork and procrastination which in a sense are two sides of the same coin. Especially if the worker lives alone or is partial to pulling "all nighters," it's easy to get lost in overwork. In the long run, this does no one any good. Not only can it create health problems for the worker, such as repetitive stress injuries and exhaustion, it can affect the quality of the output.

Studies have found that telecommuters are indeed more productive than their office counterparts. They work longer hours and even take assignments on vacation and some experts believe that their dedication may be in part due to gratitude over the fact that they can work at home, even if only part-time. However, you as a manager need to reinforce the need for work-life balance because in the long run they will get more done if they are well-rested and healthy.

Some suggestions for avoiding overwork:

☐ Encourage frequent stretch breaks, at least once every hour or so. Not only does it ease the strain on muscles from repetitive motions, it also clears the brain.

☐ Just because they are working at home, doesn't mean they are under house arrest. Encourage your workers to get out at least once a day – for example, go to the park for lunch or to the gym for a workout. They need to be responsible but they're not wearing an ankle bracelet.

☐ If possible, suggest that they take their "personal clock" into account when planning their work day. We all have times of day when we're most alert, so they should do more

difficult projects then. Conversely, easier tasks, such as phone calls and emails, can be accomplished during periods of lower energy.

☐ Teach them to prioritize by labeling tasks on a scale from one to three. First priorities should be accomplished as soon as possible; priority-two duties can be completed if time permits; and third-tier items can be delegated or postponed (but not indefinitely).

☐ Encourage the employee to ask for help. If the job takes more time than initially planned, then he should be comfortable requesting an extended deadline or additional worker(s) to help ease the burden. Make sure you're available and receptive to these requests.

On the other side is procrastination. In a way it's almost worse, because once people fall into that mode, they will do almost anything to avoid work. Temptations include the TV, family and neighbors, the refrigerator and even – though this may seem hard to believe – the cat box and the laundry. The thought of work becomes so overwhelming that employee will do almost anything to avoid it. And not all people are able to overcome procrastination – some are simply not self-starters and need the stimulus of the office and coworkers to get the job done.

However, there are some tools that can help nudge telecommuters into "work" mode:

☐ **Consider their office an "office."** That is, get up at a certain time, get dressed and be at their desk at set hours. Take a regular lunch and stretch breaks and make a commitment to doing this the days they're supposed to be working. They can even dress business casual at home to get into "office" mode.

☐ **Have teleworkers come into the office part-time.** Along with keeping motivated and "in the loop," they will have social interactions and contact with coworkers, which in and of itself can be motivating. It also helps overcome the dreaded sense of isolation common to beginning telecommuters.

☐ **Set deadlines**. Even small ones can provide incentive. Breaking a large project into smaller, more manageable chunks can overcome the intimidation factor. Detailed work plans and schedules can be especially helpful.

☐ **Provide rewards.** If the employee knows that she'll be getting a promotion or even praise by accomplishing tasks in a timely manner, then that can serve as a motivator, as well.

Overcoming Isolation

Case Study

Mary Ellen (not her real name), a video editor and a new mother, thought working from home would be the ideal arrangement, allowing her to be close to her son all day. However, once she began, she found it frustrating and lonely, and it was difficult to concentrate. "I missed the atmosphere of the office and my coworkers," she admitted. "I'm an extrovert who gets energy from people around me, they help start the ideas flowing … Working from home basically turned off my creative faucet."

Although this may not be so much the case with teleworkers at, say, a company when they are constantly on the phone, some people simply cannot work alone. And they may not find this out until they are actually in the situation, with just them and the same four walls, day in and day out.

However, there are steps you can take to help them overcome a sense of isolation.

Keep them in the loop. "Telecommuters have a heightened need to feel included," observes author Lin Grensing-Pophal. "When you share information with them, they will feel more involved in what's happening at the company." This can take the form of an informal luncheon, a fellow worker's going-away party, or something as simple as informing them about the organization's long-range plans.

Create an atmosphere where the team can connect regularly, be it virtually, through conference calls or even meeting face-to-face. Consistent contact and a sense of camaraderie with peers go a long way in eliminating feelings of isolation.

Encourage the worker to pursue professional development and training. Depending upon the company's policies, you might provide partial or full reimbursement. New knowledge and brainstorming with colleagues helps inspire and motivate workers.

If the worker is remote to the company, suggest that he network with professional or social organizations related to the job or even his hobbies. This can be anything from meeting regularly for lunch with those in the same field, or taking up a social sport, such as tennis or softball.

Provide the option of working part-time in the office, or going back full-time for a designated period. This was touched upon in the previous section, but if the sense of isolation continues or worsens, "office time" might need to be increased, or perhaps be made permanent.

Growing Telework in Your Organization

Expand and Develop Your Network

The Bureau of Labor Statistics report reveals that the likelihood of people working at home varies greatly based on the industry. For example, 30 percent of those employed in management, professional and related occupations regularly conduct work at home. Almost two-thirds of those who usually worked at home are employed in these fields. Twenty percent of sales workers report usually working at home. Conversely, only about three percent of those employed in production, transportation and the material-moving field reported working at home. One-third of people who reported usually working at home are self-employed. The percentage of men and women who work at home is nearly equal while those who are married, who have children or who are college graduates are more likely to work at home than their counterparts.

Source: hubpages.com

As individuals and companies struggle to reduce their carbon footprint and gas prices continue to rise, these figures will likely continue to increase. Market forecasters, such as the Yankee Group, Gartner and Nielson's, estimated the total number of U.S. telecommuters will escalate to about 50 million by 2010, with similar patterns of growth in Europe, Canada, Japan, and elsewhere.

But where will these workers come from? Author Harriet Hankin, in her book The New Workforce identifies five emerging trends.

- ☐ **An increasingly aging yet active population:** Lifestyle changes and medical advances keep people alive and fit into their 90s, according to the book. Financial pressures and personal desire are also motivators. Nowhere is this more evident than at ARO, where many employees are Baby Boomers or younger retirees. This was not by design; rather, the jobs themselves fit their needs and schedules.

- ☐ **The decline of the nuclear family and the rise of alternative households:** Today the traditional two-parent, 2.5 child family is but a slice of the workforce pie, which also consists of single parents, same-sex partners, stay-at-home dads, and grandparents raising grandkids, among many others. Companies will need to develop benefits programs, flexible schedules, and make other accommodations to meet their varied requirements.

- ☐ **A workplace that also is becoming more racially diverse and blended:** Race, ethnicity, religion, gender, sexual orientation, and even nationality come into play here. Thanks to technology, virtual teams can work from anywhere, using anyone who has

the proper skills. Along with obvious racial, religious, and other differences, companies need to become attuned to the disparity in cultures as they expand globally.

☐ **Multiple generations working side by side:** This starts with the Silent Generation (born before 1946) and extends through Baby Boomers (born from 1946-64), Gen X (1965 to late 1970s); and Gen Y, Nexters, and Millennials, various gradations of whom were born after 1980. Each generation has its own code of values, needs, expectations, and styles of work. Savvy companies will understand these differences, using the strengths of each to achieve their goals.

☐ **The understanding that it's more than a paycheck,** or even a long-term commitment:

Telecommuters in particular are concerned with work-life balance – otherwise they wouldn't be working remotely. And like their office peers, they look for management that champions trust, mutual respect, and ethical conduct.

The days of supervising employees through fear and punishment have gone the way of the gold watch for 30 years of service to a single company. According to the Bureau of Labor Statistics, the average person born during the later years of the Baby Boom held 10.5 jobs from the ages of 18-40, although nearly three-fifths of the job changes occurred before age 25.

These trends speak volumes about how companies need to re-think the traditional way of hiring, training, and retaining employees. Telecommuters are an increasingly large part of this picture.

Growing use of virtual teams

Certain types of virtual workers are more and more in demand. Although some parts of the economy are suffering, those with skills ranging from customer service to information technology (IT) can basically work from anywhere, anytime. This trend makes it harder for smaller firms to compete in terms of salary and benefits packages.

Thus, the stage is set for telecommuting, an ideal arrangement for those with the right "personality" and training. Gartner, the Stamford, CT technology research and advisory company, predicts that by 2015, IT people will spend more than 80 percent of their time working collaboratively, often across 10 or more virtual teams. However, many of their findings can be applied to other in-demand workers, as well.

According to Gartner, six emerging rules will govern the workplace of the future: The quality of peers will matter.

☐ The competition for qualified talent will be global.

☐ The employment model will change shape.

☐ No two people will approach work in the same way.

☐ Talented people will move around.

☐ Physical gaps between leaders and followers will widen.

Adapted from: www.cio.co.uk

Remember During the next 5-10 years, knowledge workers in particular will increasingly utilize a combination of global communication and personal devices, as well as location-independent technologies, such as blogs and Wikis. Even today, informal social networks, such as interactive Websites allow international groups of professionals to exchange information and job tips. So to recruit qualified team members, companies may find themselves switching from local to globally-based job searches.

Gartner also predicts that, while businesses traditionally defined and supplied workers' technology and equipment, "technically savvy" telecommuters will be purchasing and choosing their own hardware and software to collaborate and meet goals and deadlines. This jibes with the results-oriented culture of the telecommuter, in which product and not process is what counts.

As technology becomes more sophisticated and interactive, various glitches and discrepancies between incompatible programs and devices will be smoothed over. An example is the former incompatibility between Windows and Mac-based applications. Even Apple's Website provides tips and information on how users of both can connect to the same networks, share common applications, and exchange data and files.

Looking Ahead

No one knows what the future holds. But it looks to be bright for teleworkers and, by extension, their managers. No longer the punitive watchdog who must scrutinize their workers' every move, managers can focus on getting the best possible results from employees who are not only motivated to get the job done but happier and more productive.

Many of the negative things about an office – the pettiness, the physical discomfort of having to work in a uniform environment, the rigid schedules, not to mention the commute – are eliminated by telecommuting. And as technology evolves, many of the glitches that have occurred in the past will be resolved, although undoubtedly some new ones will take their place.

Although telecommuting is not for every job, trends and forecasts indicate that it will become more and more commonplace. So, while it may not be in your immediate future, it behooves at least some consideration and study since you may find yourself in a remote management position – with or without teleworkers – sooner, rather than later.

SUMMARY: EFFECTIVELY MANAGING TELEWORKERS

In many ways, managing telecommuters is the same as managing office workers. You will likely find that you're calling upon the same skills and experience when setting performance standards, assigning workload, doing scheduling, and so forth.

Must Do

However, there are important – and challenging -- differences. For one thing, by focusing on results, instead of processes, you must become an effective communicator, one who is versatile and well-versed in the different methods of exchanging information, be it phone or email, real-time videoconferencing or use of Intranets and electronic bulletin boards. This may require a considerable investment of time and effort, especially when it comes to setting up channels of contact with virtual employees, each of whom has their own preferred methods and personal communication strengths. Still, if they don't know exactly what you mean, how can they be expected to perform the job?

An added complexity in dealing with telecommuters is measuring productivity. So much more than the traditional counting of widgets produced each hour, many factors come into play: Is the person doing the job better, even if it takes more time? What will the long-term results be? How do you measure customer satisfaction? And of course, the issues caused by technology, whether it is actually helping or hindering your organization's goals and how it affects worker performance.

Tips

Finally, you'll need to set a schedule for regular feedback, with you, your employees and the team in general. This can take the form of face-to-face meetings, conference calls, or the various modes of virtual communication. In addition to soliciting their comments and opinions, as well as making sure that everyone (office, support, and remote workers) is apprised of what's currently happening with projects and processes, problems will need to be addressed immediately and directly.

For instance, a situation may arise that requires telling the employee outright that the continuation of telecommuting (or even his job) is dependent upon him improving his performance. Of course, you'll want to hear his side of the story, as well. Regardless of what ensues, the conversation should be both solution and results-oriented.

Author Lin Grensing-Pophal lists additional qualities important in managing telecommuters:

- ☐ **Comfort with supervising a remote workforce:** This is a threshold issue. Many managers simply cannot overcome their perceived need to keep employees in their sight.

- ☐ **Understanding what is required of the position:** The manager must clearly know the requirements of the position and be able to quantify or measure the output expected from the position.

- ☐ **Ability to clearly articulate goals and objectives:** Telecommuters must know what is expected of them. Management must be able to outline, specifically, the expectations and job standards that the telecommuter will be expected to meet.

- ☐ **Effective interpersonal communication:** Communication is the key to a successful telecommuting relationship. Managers must establish means of interacting with the telecommuter, and allowing the telecommuter to interact with the rest of the staff through both face-to-face and technological methods.

- ☐ **Ability to provide clear and consistent feedback:** Managers must be willing and able to provide telecommuters with frequent and specific feedback. At any sign that the relationship is not working, or that objectives are not being met, the manager must immediately address the situation and, if necessary, rethink the approach.

Source: Telecommuting: Managing Offsite Staff for Small Business, p. 135

Understanding these characteristics and being comfortable with management by results can provide a basis or starting point for effective workload planning.

Clarify Expectations and Standards for the Entire Team

Tips

When your organization decides to offer a telework program, your employees will have a lot of questions. Bring them all together whether or not they plan to telework because it is important that everyone hears the same message, right from the start.

Make sure from the beginning that everyone is aware that teleworking doesn't change the organization's business focus. Stress that teleworking is not a perk or an entitlement but a way for employees to be more productive and performance-oriented, while providing opportunities for better work/life balance. Everyone needs to understand their job responsibilities; for instance, deadlines remain the same even if you are working remotely.

Summary: Effectively Managing Teleworkers

Establish ground rules and procedures that ensure productivity and collaboration. Discuss your communication needs and clarify procedures, such as how to know if it's someone's telework day. Take time to walk through the company's telework policy and guidelines, and review eligibility criteria.

Spend time talking about what can go wrong. Telework introduces new ways of working together; encourage your employees to think about potential problems before they happen.

Complete a Telework Agreement for Each Telework Employee

Tips

Most organizations have a Telework Agreement, as detailed in earlier chapters. As a manager, you'll find the agreement to be an invaluable tool for guiding your discussion with the prospective teleworker, and for recording his or her commitments. Ideally, the manager and the employee will first have a thorough conversation about the employee's job responsibilities, including how to perform well as a teleworker.

Rather than being a performance plan, the agreement documents the specific arrangements and agreements between the manager and the employee. It will include things, such as how many days per week or pay period the employee can telework, their core hours, and clarification on what the company will pay for (such as a laptop, business phone, Internet service, etc.), versus what the employee must provide. Both parties, supervisor and employee, must sign the agreement.

Communicate Regularly for Productivity and Performance

Must Do

Measuring your employees' performance isn't about seeing them busily active – it's about seeing real results. Whether or not your employees are teleworkers, they should be clear on their job responsibilities and deliverables. Teleworkers must plan their work carefully to ensure they are productive both at home and in the office. Be very specific about how you want to be kept informed about their accomplishments. Talk with your teleworkers about meaningful measures of productivity, and the results you expect to see in terms of productivity, quality, and timeliness. Spend plenty of time on key measures of performance, such as effectiveness in communications, planning, and collaboration.

Tips

Rather than waiting for a formal evaluation period, provide consistent and frequent communication and feedback. Feedback is important for your employees so that they can improve and/or know that they are on track. And even though there's a physical distance between you and your telework employees, you can provide routine feedback through emails, phone calls or faxes. Use face-to-face meetings for significant feedback, as well as relationship- and trust-building.

Consider Tools for Efficiency and Collaboration

Tips

Investigate hardware and software solutions that might help your team communicate and work together effectively when in different locations. Bring the team together to assess the nature of their work, and the kind of communication tools they need. Are group sessions important for exploring ideas? Do you need information-sharing tools, or project-management interaction? Depending on your needs, these solutions could range from larger-scale tools, such as installing videoconferencing facilities, to simpler things, such as setting up a team Website or project message center for general information sharing. You may want to add a chat room or discussion area to your Website, as well. Be sure to include your IT experts as you strategize solutions, so they can help with integration and security. Arrange for training, if necessary, to ensure your team's ability to use any new tools you introduce.

Maintain Harmony in the Office

Must Do

As a manager, do your best to maintain a balance between the needs of your telework and office staff. Make sure everyone receives fair, equitable treatment regardless of where they work. Avoid singling out one group over the other.

Here are some suggestions for achieving balance:

- ☐ Keep everyone in the loop through email messages and a computer calendar system.

- ☐ Encourage healthy partnerships among all team members; consider opportunities for mentoring and cross-training, and be sure to reward good examples of collaboration.

- ☐ Hold meaningful meetings and use business reasons to determine when teleworkers should be physically present.

- ☐ Clearly communicate rules for things that apply equally to teleworkers and non-teleworkers, such as vacation, sick leave, and overtime.

- ☐ Keep communication open and provide guidance at all times. Be ready to react quickly and appropriately if there's ever a breakdown; for example if the in-office staff forgets to include teleworkers in an important meeting.

Remember your teleworkers' professional development.

Many potential teleworkers have real concerns that they'll miss important opportunities if they're not in the office every day. Others may get so comfortable working without distractions at home, that they forget the importance of team participation. It's the manager's job to support the professional development of every employee. You may need to remind your teleworkers to pay more attention to their own career development when they work remotely. Encourage them to use their in-office days for face-to-face meetings, networking, and relationship building. Challenge your employees to go after assignments and opportunities

that showcase their strengths. Reward strong collaboration among all your employees, so they see that team synergy is critical even when working in different locations. And always be an advocate for your teleworkers. When you're focused on the work they're producing, rather than where they're doing it, you can speak up on behalf of their successes.

Acknowledge Your Employees' Achievements

If telework is having a positive impact on your employees, the team, and the work you all do, let people know! Connect your appreciation to results: individual accountability, productivity, performance, and collaboration. Help employees work through change, and acknowledge their successes. Share the positive impact of your telework program with peers and senior management, too — make sure you present your successes in terms of how they specifically benefit the organization.

Tips

Other Things to Keep in Mind

Successful telework arrangements meet both management's and employees' needs. Consider the work habits and the job tasks to be completed while teleworking.

Remember

☐ Develop telework agreements that give you and your employees a clear understanding of the key terms and conditions of the work arrangements.

☐ Depending on agency requirements, telework agreements can take the form of an oral, email, or written agreement. A written agreement is most desirable.

☐ Telework agreements are not permanent and can be time-limited, modified, or canceled as needed.

☐ Manage your employees by results, whether teleworkers or not. Focus on the final product rather than processes used to produce it.

☐ Collaborate with your teleworkers and their coworkers to set work schedules. Develop work plans and task schedules based on input from the entire team.

☐ Be specific about what, where, when, and to what degree the work will be completed.

☐ Work to keep communication flowing between your teleworkers, office workers, and customers.

☐ Monitor your teleworkers' productivity, using a variety of measures.

☐ Ensure that technology requirements are identified and addressed.

Checklist

REFERENCES

Federal Employee's Emergency Guide
   Office of Personnel Management
   http://www.opm.gov/emergency/PDF/EmployeesGuide.pdf

Federal Information Security Management Act (FISMA)
   http://csrc.nist.gov/groups/SMA/fisma/index.html

Federal Management Regulation (FMR) Bulletin 2006-B3 Guidelines for Alternative
Workplace Arrangements
   Link to FMR Bulletin No. 2006-B3

Federal Manager's/Decision Maker's Emergency Guide
   Office of Personnel Management
   http://www.opm.gov/emergency/PDF/ManagersGuide.pdf

Federal Continuity Directive (FDC) 1
   http://www.fema.gov/pdf/about/offices/fcd1.pdf

GAO-03-679, July 2003
Report to the Chairman, Committee on Government Reform, House of Representatives
Human Capital: Further Guidance, Assistance, and Coordination Can Improve Federal
Telework Efforts
   http://www.gao.gov/new.items/d03679.pdf

GAO-06-713, May 2006
Report to the Chairman, Committee on Government Reform, House of Representatives
Continuity of Operations: Selected Agencies Could Improve Planning for Use of Alternate
Facilities and Telework during Disruptions
   http://www.gao.gov/new.items/d06713.pdf

National Strategy for Pandemic Influenza Implementation Plan
   http://www.whitehouse.gov/homeland/pandemic-influenza.html

NIST Special Publication 800-46 Revision 1
    Guide to Enterprise Telework and Remote Access Security
    http://csrc.nist.gov/publications/nistpubs/800-46-rev1/sp800-46r1.pdf

Glossary

Client Device: A system used by a remote worker to access an organization's network and the systems on that network.

Consumer Device: A small, usually mobile computer that does not run a standard PC OS or that runs a standard PC OS, but does not permit users to access it directly. Examples of consumer devices are networking-capable personal digital assistants (PDA), cell phones, and video game systems.

Direct Application Access: A high-level remote access architecture that allows teleworkers to access an individual application directly, without using remote access software.

Personal Computer: A desktop or laptop computer running a standard PC operating system (e.g., Windows Vista, Windows XP, Linux/Unix, and Mac OS X).

Portal: A high-level remote access architecture that is based on a server that offers teleworkers access to one or more applications through a single centralized interface.

Remote Access: The ability for an organization's users to access its non-public computing resources from external locations other than the organization's facilities.

Remote Desktop Access: A high-level remote access architecture that gives a teleworker the ability to remotely control a particular desktop computer at the organization, most often the user's own computer at the organization's office, from a telework client device.

Session Locking: A feature that permits a user to lock a session upon demand or locks the session after it has been idle for a preset period of time.

Split Tunneling: A VPN client feature that tunnels all communications involving the organization's internal resources through the VPN, thus protecting them, and excludes all other communications from going through the tunnel.

Telecommuting: See "Telework."

Telework: The ability for an organization's employees and contractors to perform work from locations other than the organization's facilities.

Telework Client Device: A PC or consumer device used by a teleworker for performing telework.

Tunneling: A high-level, remote-access architecture, that provides a secure tunnel between a telework client device and a tunneling server, through which application traffic may pass.

Virtual Private Network (VPN): A virtual network, that provides a secure communications tunnel for data and other information transmitted between networks, built on top of existing physical networks.

Notes

Notes

Notes

Notes

Notes